By Gary Beck

Novels

Extreme Change
Acts of Defiance
Flawed Connections
Call to Valor
Sudden Conflicts
Wave Length

Crumbling Ramparts
Flare Up
Raise High the Walls
Still Defiant
State of Rage

Poetry

Expectations
Days of Destruction
Dawn in Cities
Assault on Nature
Songs of a Clerk
Civilized Ways
Conditioned Response
Displays
Resonance
Perceptions
Fault Lines
Tremors
Virtual Living
Perturbations

Blossoms of Decay
Rude Awakenings
Blunt Force
The Remission of Order
Contusions
Transitions
Earth Links
Mortal Coil
Desperate Seeker
Too Harsh For Pastels
Temporal Dreams
Severance
Redemption Value
Fractional Disorder

Play Collections
The Big Match and other one act plays
Collected Plays of Gary Beck Volume I
Plays of Aristophanes translated then directed by Gary Beck

Short Story Collections
A Glimpse of Youth
Now I Accuse and other stories
Dogs Don't Send Flowers and other stories

Essays
Collected Essays of Gary Beck

Three Plays

By Aristophanes.

Translated by

Gary Beck and Jane Oliensis

Dedication

To Nancy, Autry, Julann, Sherry and the other talented actors who delighted audiences at our theatre and on tour with wonderful performances of these great comedies.

Special Thanks

To the distinguished scholar, Dr. Maurice Charney, for his review of the translations and his lectures to the actors on ancient Greek comedy and culture, which contributed to the quality of the performances.

To the excellent scholar, Dr. Peter Gruen, whose comprehensive work with the actors on ancient Greek comedy and culture helped bring the plays to life for contemporary audiences.

To Jane Oliensis for her fine translation collaboration with Gary Beck that prepared these plays for the stage, not the classroom.

Translator's Note by Gary Beck

The three plays were translated for stage production. Ms. Oliensis did the basic texts. Our consulting scholars, Dr. Charney and Dr. Gruen made sure we respected the classical elements of the plays. I made the structure and dialog suitable for the stage, while maintaining the integrity of the original. Anyone who knows the comedies of Aristophanes wants a text that has spirit and liveliness. Lysistrata was only performed at our theater due to its strong sexual content. Women in Assembly and The Birds had a full six week run at our theater and toured colleges, senior citizen centers, underserved communities and public spaces, to the delight of the spectrum of audiences.

Director's Introduction by Gary Beck

It was exciting and fun to direct the comedies of Aristophanes. I started my theater company with a ten year plan. First Commedia del' arte, a cycle of Moliere, then Aristophanes and in our seventh year our first hit show. I performed in most of the productions when I couldn't get an older actor to play the old fool. The older capable actors wanted more money than I could afford. The retreads, the retirees from IBM, G.E., Ford, who decided to become actors after 25 years of corporate servitude didn't have the drive of a true actor and lacked the skills, abilities and techniques that actors acquired over the years.

The company I formed was based on an ensemble concept, developed during a complex and demanding rehearsal process. This was not suitable for most actors conditioned to the Showcase system of limited rehearsals, 12 performances over three weekends, with the caveat that an actor could leave the show at any time for paid work. So if a producer put all his money into the hope of an Off-Broadway production, his lead actor could depart for a tv commercial, ending the production.

My path to Aristophanes started with Commedia, fast-paced farce with elements of high culture and low buffoonery. Moliere, who started as a commedia actor, was a transition away from low comedy, though still related. The last Moliere play I directed, Two Pretentious Maidens Ridiculed, was an almost mannerist comedy, with highly developed characters that moved audiences of all types to laughter.

Aristophanes was far more appealing to my personal taste and directorial interest. The plays are social, political, creative expressions of the Athenian culture that shaped the playwright. The plays are formally structured with a chorus of 24, inconceivable for my productions, prepared for a small Off-Broadway theater and touring. I assigned lines to individuals, rather then a ritual chorus. This brought the drama to contemporary audience sensibility and gave the actors more scope and stage life. Classical scholars talked to the company about Athenian history, culture and mythology, which gave the actors a platform to build their characters. A lengthy rehearsal process brought the actors together in the world of the play, which became a living fabric, urgent, controlled, creating vibrant performances.

The company was so deeply involved in the play that they took our audiences with them from the first entrance. Unlike Commedia and Moliere, these were issue plays. Women in Assembly had the women take over the state because the men made such a mess of it. The Birds has two old Athenians flee the corruption of Athens and exploit the birds into making a kingdom to replace the gods. Lysistrata was my personal favorite because it's an anti-war play and for a change I played a young vigorous character. Lysistrata was the only play we didn't tour due to the sexual elements that were only appropriate in a protected theater environment, where the content was just part of the play.

Lysistrata, the ancient Greek comedy, was our first hit show. We did six shows a week for six weeks in our 125 seat theater, sold out all the performances, had standing room on the weekends and turned away 50 or 60 patrons every show. We spent an enormous amount of money producing the show and paying actors and techs $100 a week, an unheard of amount at the time. Yet we earned it back at the box office. The show was bawdy, strongly acted with great conviction that transported the audience and brought them into the action appropriately, sometimes delightfully with improvisation. We were looking for a 299 seat theater when circumstances beyond our control forced us to close the show.

Hopefully these translations will be used by other directors to engage and entertain audiences.

Table of Contents

The Women in Assembly

In front of the house of Praxagora.

(Enter Praxagora).

Praxagora: (to the audience). If you can keep my secret, you'll be

a confidante to the conspiracy my friends and I

planned at the 'Festival of the Parasol'.... (Looks

around). But none of the women are here yet,

although it's getting late. Soon the Assembly will

meet and the women must take their seats without

being noticed. What happened to them? Perhaps

they couldn't get false beards? What if they couldn't

get out of the house with their husbands' clothes?...

Someone is coming. I'd better hide until I know if it's

a man or a woman.

(Enter 1st Woman).

1st Woman: It's almost time to go to the assembly. (Praxagora

joins her).

Praxagora: I've been waiting all night for you. Now that you're

here, we'll get my neighbor…. Shh, we don't want to

wake her husband.

(Enter 2nd Woman).

2nd Woman: I heard you. I've been trying to get away for an hour.

My husband's a sailor, and he even rows in his sleep.

He dreams that I'm a boat, and he gets me tied up in

the sheets. I had a hard time getting out of the

house.

(Enter Women).

Praxagora: Here come the others.

3rd Woman: I had a terrible time getting away. My husband

stuffed himself like a pig at dinner, and tossed and

turned all night. But I'm here!

Praxagora: Did you bring the beards? (Woman displays the

beards). Now it's time to finalize our plans, for the

assembly will convene soon.

1st Woman: We'd better hurry.

2nd Woman: I'll just run inside to get my knitting.

Praxagora: Knitting?

2nd Woman: Yes. I can knit while we sit in the Assembly. My

children need new clothes.

Praxagora: Knitting indeed! We're pretending to be men, and

that would give us away. We must be very clever

actors if we hope to take over the leadership of the

state. We've seen actors become leaders before, and they always fool the people for a while, until they ruin the government.

1ˢᵗ Woman: How will we debate politics as well as the men?

Praxagora: Women are natural speakers.

1ˢᵗ Woman: But we're inexperienced. We'll make mistakes.

Praxagora: That's why we're meeting early, so we can rehearse together. Now put on your beards, and we'll practice speaking. (To 2ⁿᵈ Woman). What are you giggling at?

2ⁿᵈ Woman: My beard tickles, and everyone looks so funny.

Praxagora: Stop joking. Let's begin. Who wishes to address the assembly?

1ˢᵗ Woman: I do.

Praxagora: Then speak.

1ˢᵗ Woman: First I need a drink of wine.

Praxagora: That's enough. You wouldn't say that in the assembly.

1st Woman: Don't men drink there?

Praxagora: Still talking about drinking?

1st Woman: I'm sure they do. And more than wine! Just look at

the laws they pass and it's obvious they must be

drunk most of the time. Imagine cutting off

government support for the elderly! What will

happen to my poor mother and father?

Praxagora: You're no use at all. We'll try someone else.

1st Woman: By the Gods, I wish I'd never put on a beard. It's

made me so thirsty that I can't think of anything else

but drink!

Praxagora: Who else wants to speak?

2nd Woman: I do.

Praxagora: Then speak up confidently, like a man. We don't have

much time left.

2nd Woman: I wish a more experienced speaker had brought up

this matter, and spared me from exposing a terrible

abuse. But since no one else has protested, I must.
The taverns are diluting their wine with water, and
this must stop! By the Goddesses....

Praxagora: By the Goddesses! You dolt! Have you lost your

mind?

2nd Woman: What's wrong? I didn't ask for a drink.

Praxagora: Men don't swear by the Goddesses! But except for

that slip you did very well.

2nd Woman: I meant by Apollo.

Praxagora: Try to understand that if everything isn't done

properly our plan won't work.

2nd Woman: Let me go again. I have a good idea. Listen to me, all

you assembled women....

Praxagora: Wrong again! We're men, and you call us women.

That's enough from you. I must speak for us. "I pray

the Gods will favor our plan. My friends, I am a

citizen as deeply concerned as any of you in our

country's fate. And I am disturbed at seeing the miseries facing our nation. For I see the state selecting leaders who do not care enough about the sufferings of the people. One day our leaders promise something good; the next day they do ten things wrong. We try new leaders, and they're worse than the old. It is difficult to reason with men who are so blind. Those who are well-off no longer care about those who do without."

3rd Woman: By Aphrodite, well said!

Praxagora: You fool, you must swear by male Gods. How would "By Aphrodite" sound in the Assembly?

3rd Woman: I wouldn't say it there.

Praxagora: Then don't say it here. "When they decide on foreign alliances they tell us we must be friends with this state and that, yet they never seem to be our friends. We must have ships to defend the national interest,

yet our leaders propose expensive, giant ships that
need more sailors than we have, instead of
economical, fast ships to do the job properly. Each
day it becomes harder to know who to trust.

1st Woman: This man's a clever speaker!

Praxagora: That's right. "But you, citizens of Athens, are the true
cause of our problems. You earn enough to get
comfortable and you only care about remaining
comfortable, so you forget your obligations to the
nation, which lurches along like a drunkard. But trust
my advice and we may yet be saved. I propose that
we entrust the rulership of the state to the women.
Don't they manage their households efficiently?"

2nd Woman: It's true, by Zeus. Tell us more, sir.

Praxagora: "I shall now demonstrate woman's superiority to
man. First: They wash their delicate clothes in warm
water as their mothers did, and they don't try every

new fad. And wouldn't the nation flourish if we followed our traditional values? They cook and clean as of old. They carry groceries and babies as of old. They nag their husbands as their mothers did. They hide their lovers in the closet as their mothers did. They eat candy and drink too much when their husbands are away, as their mothers did. They are thrilled at being passionately desired, as of old. Therefore, honorable citizens, let us entrust the affairs of the government to the women, and not ask too many questions about what they'll do with it. We can be certain that being politician-mothers they'll be concerned with the fate of their sons. Who could feed the nation better than women who understand the kitchen? And as for being tricked by others, who will better discover deception than women, who are famous for being deceivers? I need not say more.

Give power to the women and you'll be happy for

the rest of your life."

1st Woman: O wonderful speech, sweetest Praxagora. Where did

you learn to talk like that?

Praxagora: When the Spartans chased everyone from the

countryside into Athens, my husband and I stayed in

the Assembly. I learned by listening to the orators.

1st Woman: You are so clever. We women appoint you leader of

the nation. But what if the men don't agree with

your plan?

Praxagora: I'll say they're demented.

2nd Woman: What if they try to throw you out?

Praxagora: I'll resist them.

1st Woman: And we'll help you. But what about voting? We're

more accustomed to spreading our legs than raising

our arms.

Praxagora: An important point. Don't forget the proper way. You
lift one hand straight up, and bare your arm to the
shoulder. Now put on your husband's cloaks and
fasten your beards securely, and let's be off to the
Assembly.

2nd Woman: (to the Women). Let's go. Many other women will
join us there.

Praxagora: Hurry then. Remember, only those who get to the
Assembly early enough get paid for attending. (Exit
Women).

(Enter Blepyros).

Blepyros: What's the world coming to? Where's my wife? It's
almost time to go to the Assembly and I can't budge
my bowels! I called the comforter of my old age to
prepare an enema for me, and she was nowhere to

be found! And I can't even find my cloak! I wanted to find a private place to squat and strain and get rid of some excess dung, but there are citizens everywhere! Ohh, my belly.... What a fool I was to get married in my old age. I should be publicly whipped. She's always tormenting me, and what mischief she's up to now, the Gods alone know.

(Enter Cinesias).

Cinesias: Who is this here? Surely not my good neighbor Blepyros? By Zeus, it is. Greetings, old friend. What's wrong?

Blepyros: Nothing. I'm just getting some air and looking for my cloak.

Cinesias: Why don't you have your wife look for it?

Blepyros: I can't find her! She snuck out somewhere and I've

got a feeling she's up to no good.

Cinesias: By Poseidon, the same thing's happened to me. My

wife's gone and so's my cloak.

Blepyros: I just came out to fart and I can't even do that with

all these citizens around.

Cinesias: Well, where is she? Did one of her friends invite her

to breakfast?

Blepyros: That must be it. She's a good wife. She wouldn't do

anything wrong. At least I don't think she would.

Cinesias: Are your bowels rumbling? But I must get to the

Assembly, as soon as I find my cloak. It's the only one

I own. (Exit Cinesias).

Blepyros: I'll meet you there.... As soon as my bowels stop

aching! By Zeus, what pain! How'll I ever eat again? I

need a doctor! Is there someone here who could

cure me? A specialist in turd removal? No one? Oh,

you immortal gods, I beseech you, ease my bowels of

their pain, so I may eat again!

(Enter Chremes).

Chremes: Greetings, friend. What's ailing you?

Blepyros: I'm constipated! But I'm all right. Where are you

                coming from?

Chremes: From the assembly.

Blepyros: Is it over already?

Chremes: Yes, by Zeus! Today it ended almost before it began.

Blepyros: What happened?

Chremes: It was very strange. A whole crowd of newcomers

                with funny looking beards filled the place, so we

                couldn't get in.

Blepyros: What was such a crowd doing there so early?

Chremes: The Magistrates decided to let the Assembly vote on
the best plan for the safety of the nation. One of our
friends got up to make the first speech, and the
newcomers yelled out that he was a drunken lout
who could barely find the Assembly, let alone guide
the fate of Athens. Then another friend stood up and
said that thieves were making off with the wealth of
Athens, and this very morning his cloak was stolen.
Then others yelled: mine too, mine too!" But they
were shouted down.

Blepyros: What happened next?

Chremes: Then a young fellow with a funny beard jumped up,
and made a speech demanding that we give control
of the government to the women. Some of his
supporters cheered, and our friends booed loudly.

Blepyros: I'm glad there were some folk there with sense.
Imagine trusting the women.

Chremes: But there weren't enough protests, so the youth

continued and said a lot of good things about the

women, and some terrible things about you.

Blepyros: Me? What did he say?

Chremes: First he said you were a scoundrel and a loafer.

Blepyros: He didn't! What did he say about you?

Chremes: I'll come to that. Next he said you were a thief.

Blepyros: Only me?

Chremes: Then he said you were a liar and a cheat, along with

most of the other citizens here.

Blepyros: I can't deny that.

Chremes: Then he went on saying women were clever and

thrifty, and knew how to keep a secret. Not like you

and me, who babble state secrets to foreigners.

Blepyros: By Hermes, he's right about that.

Chremes: Then he said that women lent each other valuables,

clothes, jewelry, money, and they didn't need

witnesses or papers, and they always kept their word
and repaid their debts. While men are always
quarreling and going to the law-courts to settle
disputes.

Blepyros: By Zeus! That's true. Even though there are
witnesses.

Chremes: Then they don't inform on their neighbors, they
don't bring lawsuits, and they support democracy.
He praised women for many other fine qualities.

Blepyros: What happened then?

Chremes: It was decided that the women will rule the nation.
For we've tried everything else, and nothing has
solved our problems.

Blepyros: Is it official?

Chremes: Certainly.

Blepyros: And now they're in charge of everything?

Chremes: Everything.

Blepyros: Then my wife's the boss now?

Chremes: Yes, and she rules the house.

Blepyros: And she'll get up grouchy in the morning to take care

of affairs of state?

Chremes: Yes. From now on that's the woman's job. You must

stay home and tend the house.

Blepyros: It just dawned on me. Now that the women have

power, what will we older men do when they try to

force us to....

Chremes: To do what?

Blepyros: To go to bed with them?

Chremes: What if we can't?

Blepyros: Then they won't give us any breakfast.

Chremes: So we must perform to earn our breakfast.

Blepyros: I won't be forced! I won't!

Chremes: We must obey. If that's what we must do for the

public good, we must do our duty cheerfully. There's

an old saying: However silly our laws, the Gods help

us endure to the end. May it be so now, o Goddesses

of Athens. I must be off, old friend. Goodbye. (Exit

Chremes).

Blepyros: Farewell, Chremes. (Exit Blepyros).

(Enter Praxagora and Women, coming from the Assembly).

Chorus: Hurry, hurry! Are any men following us from the

Assembly? Look around! Be on your guard! For men

are treacherous brutes. If they thought we tricked

them, they would punish us. That would be

disgraceful, so be alert. This is where we met before

we went to the Assembly. And there is the house of

our new Princess-President, who devised the

splendid plan that has become the new law. Let us

salute our new leader!... But we are risking

everything by lingering in disguise, for if discovered

we'll be denounced as criminals. Let's get rid of our

beards and cloaks, and show ourselves as women....

How itchy that filthy bird's nest was! How hot under

my husband's cloak.

Praxagora: O Women of Athens, you see how well our hopes

have turned to facts. But now get rid of your

husband's cloaks and staffs, before any of the men

see you. You. (to a Servant). Put this cloak and staff

near my husband's side of the bed.

Chorus: Everything you told us to do is done. Now you must

instruct us further, if we are to obey properly. For I

have never listened to such a clever woman!

Praxagora: Then I appoint all of you advisors to the state. For in

the planning and struggle you've been brave and

resourceful. (Enter Blepyros from the house).

Blepyros: It's you! Where have you been, Praxagora?

Praxagora: What difference does it make, my dear?

Blepyros: What difference does it make? Are you demented?

Praxagora: You don't think I was with a lover.

Blepyros: Probably more than one!

Praxagora: You can test me.

Blepyros: How?

Praxagora: See if I smell of perfume.

Blepyros: What does that prove? Can't a woman see her lover

              without perfume?

Praxagora: I wouldn't.

Blepyros: They why did you sneak off so early with my cloak?

Praxagora: A good friend who was ready to have a baby

              summoned me during the night.

Blepyros: Why didn't you tell me where you were going?

Praxagora: It was an emergency! I had to rush away.

Blepyros: And you couldn't tell me? You're up to some

              mischief!

Praxagora: By the Goddesses! I rushed out immediately, just as I
was. The messenger begged me to hurry.

Blepyros: Why didn't you wear your own clothes? You took my
cloak and staff, and left me stretched out snoring
loud enough to wake the dead, only you didn't finish
me off.

Praxagora: But it was cold, and I am thin and delicate, and so
helpless, so I took your cloak to keep me warm, and
left you snug and cozy in bed, dearest husband.

Blepyros: Do you know that you cost us a half-bushel of wheat
that I would have earned at the Assembly?

Praxagora: Don't be concerned, for she had a baby boy.

Blepyros: The Assembly?

Praxagora: No, by Zeus! My woman friend! Has the Assembly
met?

Blepyros: Yes, by Zeus! Don't you remember? I told you about
it yesterday.

Praxagora: O, yes. Now I remember.

Blepyros: Then you haven't heard about the new law that was

               passed?

Praxagora: By Zeus, I haven't.

Blepyros: Well get ready for a surprise. The state has been

               entrusted to your hands.

Praxagora: To do what? To knit?

Blepyros: By Zeus. No! To rule.

Praxagora: To rule what?

Blepyros: The affairs of state, big and small.

Praxagora: By Aphrodite, the state will be happy from now on!

Blepyros: Why?

Praxagora: For many reasons. Rascals will no longer be

               permitted to abuse the state; no one will be a false

               witness; no one will betray their neighbors.

Blepyros: By the Gods, don't do this, for it would mean the end

               of my livelihood.

Chorus: Honored sir, allow your wife to speak.

Praxagora: No one will steal clothes, or envy one's neighbor, or
               be naked, or poor, or insult others, or seize a
               debtor's property.

Chorus: By Poseidon, what if this were true?

Praxagora: It is. I will prove it, and you'll be my witnesses if this
               man contradicts me.

Chorus: Now it's time to show your support of the common
               people who will help you enforce the new laws. Your
               cleverness will help our city prosper. It's necessary,
               for our state needs a plan to survive. Think of
               something new and different. Don't delay. Tell us
               quickly, so we may admire you.

Praxagora: I am confident that I shall do what's right. But I'm
               afraid our fellow citizens won't try anything new.

Blepyros: Don't be afraid to make changes. Athenians say: Out
               with the old, in with the new.

Praxagora: Now don't interrupt me until I finish explaining the

new laws. I proclaim universal sharing. Let everyone

share their property with their neighbors. We'll have

no more rich or poor. No more great estates owned

by one man, while others haven't six feet to be

buried in. There'll be no more private property; no

more servants for some while others go unserved.

Everyone will have a basic pension, and no one will

have more than another.

Blepyros: Then everyone will have an equal share?

Praxagora: You'll eat dung first!

Blepyros: Will we dine on dung?

Praxagora: No, by Zeus! But you were the first to interrupt me. I

was about to explain the plan: first I will order that

land, money, jewels and other valuables will be held

in common. Then we'll support everyone by farming

and careful use of communal property.

Blepyros: What if someone doesn't own land, but has money?

Praxagora: He shall donate it for the public good, and if he

              cheats the state, he'll be punished.

Blepyros: He probably got his money by cheating the state.

Praxagora: That won't matter anymore.

Blepyros: Why not?

Praxagora: There'll be no more crime caused by poverty, for

              everyone will share equally: bread, meat, wine,

              warm clothes. So what good would it do to hoard

              money? You wouldn't be able to use it anymore.

Blepyros: Then won't those who are already rich try to get

              more and more?

Praxagora: That's the way it used to be, honored husband,

              under the old laws. But now, when property is

              communal, what's the advantage of not sharing?

Blepyros: What if someone sees a pretty girl and wants to

              make love to her? He can buy her presents from his

secret hoard, yet enjoy a share of communal

property by making love to her.

Praxagora: He'll be allowed to make love to her for free; for I'll

pass a law that love is free, and anyone can have

children.

Blepyros: What if everyone only wants the beautiful women?

Praxagora: The ugly shall sit next to the beautiful, and if

someone wants a beautiful woman, he must first

make love to an ugly one.

Blepyros: What about us, the old men who aren't vigorous

enough to work their way through the ugly women

to reach the beauties?

Praxagora: The beauties won't complain.

Blepyros: About what?

Praxagora: About your not making love to them. The law is

meant to keep dirty old men away from young

women.

Blepyros: What a sensible plan! You won't allow any women to

be neglected. But what will the men do? Women will

avoid the ugly ones, and only want handsome men.

Praxagora: The ugly men shall follow the handsome ones

wherever they go, and spy on them in public places.

And women won't be allowed to make love with

handsome men until they make love with the ugly

men first.

Blepyros: Then a noble old nose will be as desirable as a

handsome youth?

Praxagora: Yes, by Apollo! The plan is very democratic. It makes

an old man a rival of an athlete, for an old man can

always claim his right to be first.

Blepyros: But if we follow these laws, how will we know our

own sons?

Praxagora: What difference does it make? Children will consider

men older than themselves to be their fathers.

Blepyros: They'll strangle every old man, one by one; for even

now they strangle their real fathers, and they still

know who they are. When they don't know who's

who, they'll turd all over them.

Praxagora: Their neighbors won't allow it. Once they didn't care

if someone abused other people's fathers, but now,

if people see a father being abused, they'll stop the

abuser since it might be their father.

Blepyros: That makes sense to me. But what if a neighbor I

detest were to run after me, and call me father?

Praxagora: He was born before the new law was official, so you

don't have to worry.

Blepyros: That would have been horrible.... But who is going to

grow our food?

Praxagora: Special farmers. But that's not your concern. All you

have to do is oil yourself properly, and attend state

banquets.

Blepyros: What about clothing? What happens when our

              cloaks wear out?

Praxagora: What you have now will last a long time. Later we'll

              weave whatever we need.

Blepyros: One last question: If someone is brought into court

              on a complaint, how will he pay a fine? It isn't right

              to pay a lawsuit from the common fund.

Praxagora: You needn't worry, for there'll be no more lawsuits.

Blepyros: But this will ruin all the lawyers!

Praxagora: I'll pass a law forbidding lawsuits. Why should there

              be any, you rascal?

Blepyros: By Apollo, for many reasons! What if a man owes

              money, and refuses to pay?

Praxagora: Where did the lender get the money to lend, since all

              things are held in common? We'd convict the lender

              of theft.

Blepyros: By the Goddesses, you're teaching us well! What if

after a banquet someone is drunk, and beats and

insults people; how will he be punished? (aside). I

don't think she'll be able to answer this.

Praxagora: We'll take away his food and wine, until he behaves

properly.

Blepyros: But what about thieves?

Praxagora: There won't be any. Why should anyone steal when

they own a share of everything?

Blepyros: They won't even rob people at night?

Praxagora: Not if you behave yourself, and stay home at night.

Everyone will have a share. So if you're robbed, give

your goods to the robber willingly. Why should you

resist? Simply go to the public treasury and get

something better.

Blepyros: What about gambling?

Praxagora: There won't be any money to gamble with.

Blepyros: What will our home life be like?

Praxagora: We will all live together. For the city will be one big

               house, so anyone can go into anyone else's house.

Blepyros: Where will meals be served?

Praxagora: In the law-courts; and handsome boys shall sing

               beautiful songs about Gods and heroes, and about

               cowardly citizens who don't do their duty, so they'll

               be too ashamed to come and eat.

Blepyros: By Apollo, a fine plan! But will men and women dine

               together?

Praxagora: You dolt! Of course they will! Now tell me, do the

               new laws please you?

Blepyros: Very much.

Praxagora: Then I must pick a female herald, and be off to the

               market place where I'll receive all donated property.

               Since I have been selected to rule the nation, I must

do it properly. I have to arrange the celebration feast

so you will eat.

Blepyros: You mean we'll have a banquet today?

Praxagora: Certainly. I also have to consider new laws about the

rights of men. Farewell. (Exit Praxagora).

Blepyros: I'll meet you in the market place later. Everyone will

admire me; people will say: there is the husband of

our new Princess-President. Isn't he splendid!

(Enter Chremes, Pronomus).

Pronomus: Shall I share my property with anyone? I'd be a

wretched fool if I did that. By Poseidon, I won't! I

won't! I'll wait and see how things are going first. I

won't throw my savings away that I worked so hard

to earn. I have to see what others do.

Chremes: I'm selecting my contributions to the public treasury.

That's the new law. Haven't you heard of it?

Pronomus: You mean you're giving away your property?

Chremes: Certainly.

Pronomus: By Zeus, you are a silly fool.

Chremes: Why? Shouldn't I obey the law?

Pronomus: The law? What law?

Chremes: The law that's just been passed.

Pronomus: O, that new law. I think you are demented.

Chremes: Demented?

Pronomus: Aren't you? You're the maddest man in Athens.

Chremes: Because I obey the law?

Pronomus: Should a wise man obey laws like a sheep? That's

what fools do.

Chremes: Then you're not turning in your property?

Pronomus: I won't do anything for a while. I'll wait and see what

others do.

Chremes: What else can they do but obey the law?

Pronomus: I'll believe it when I see it.

Chremes: You can hear people discussing it in the streets.

Pronomus: All I hear is talk.

Chremes: Everyone says they're going to do it.

Pronomus: So they say.

Chremes: You doubt everything.

Pronomus: So does everyone else.

Chremes: May the Gods curse you.

Pronomus: Soon they will curse you. You don't really think that

              sane men are going to give away all they own? That's

              not natural to our way of life. By Zeus, we're meant

              to receive, not give. That's how the Gods do it. We

              know that by looking at the greedy hands of statues

              of the Gods. When we pray to them for prosperity,

              they extend their hands to get, not to give.

Chremes: You scoundrel. Let me alone. I've got work to do. I
              must get my things ready to donate to the state.

Pronomus: Then you really mean to do it?

Chremes: By Zeus, I will. I'm going to make a list of my
              property.

Pronomus: What folly! Why don't you wait to see what others
              do, and then....

Chremes: And then?

Pronomus: Why wait a little longer, and don't rush into new
              things blindly.

Chremes: Why not?

Pronomus: Because if disaster were to strike Athens, an
              earthquake, or plague, or a lightning storm, or a
              black cat crossing the marketplace bringing bad luck,
              nobody would give anything away, you dolt.

Chremes: The joke would be on me if I was the only one to give
              everything away.

Pronomus: Wait a few days, and there'll be time enough to give.

Chremes: What do you mean?

Pronomus: People sometimes vote for things quickly, but they

change their minds just as fast.

Chremes: They'll bring their things, my friend.

Pronomus: And if they don't?

Chremes: They will.

Pronomus: What if they don't?

Chremes: We'll force them in battle.

Pronomus: What if they win?

Chremes: I'll run away.

Pronomus: What if they chase you, and beat you?

Chremes: May plague take you!

Pronomus: How would that help you?

Chremes: You'd stop plaguing me.

Pronomus: You're really going to do it?

Chremes: At last you understand. I shall join my neighbors, and

obey the law.

Pronomus: Which of these misers and loafers will go with you?

Chremes: You're a hard man.

Pronomus: Hard! When every day we see the government

deciding to cut out vital services?

Chremes: By Zeus, that's true!

Pronomus: Didn't our new leaders tell us that they'd solve our

problems and give us prosperity? And now they want

to build gigantic useless ships, while all the old

people go hungry.

Chremes: That was when the men were rulers. Now that

women rule the nation, things will be different.

Pronomus: By Poseidon, they won't get the better of me.

Chremes: You're babbling nonsense. I must go about my

business.

(Enter a Female Crier).

Female Crier: Attention all citizens. Not some, but all. In accordance with the new laws, rush to the palace of our Princess-President to draw lots for places at the celebration feast. The tables are piled high with delicacies and delicious treats. The dancing girls and musicians are performing. Your friends and neighbors are already there, dining and dancing. Hurry, hurry. Rush to the feast with open mouths to taste good things. (Exit Crier).

Pronomus: I'm off to the feast. I won't waste a moment since this is the new law of the state.

Chremes: But you haven't contributed your share. Where are you going?

Pronomus: To the feast.

Chremes: They won't let you in until you pay your share.

Pronomus: I'll pay.

Chremes: When?

Pronomus: What difference does it make? It won't hurt anybody

if I'm a little late in paying.

Chremes: Yet you're still going to the feast?

Pronomus: Certainly. Good citizens must obey the laws of the

state. It is important to support the state loyally.

Chremes: What if they don't let you in?

Pronomus: I'll charge in head first.

Chremes: What if they beat you?

Pronomus: I'll have them banished.

Chremes: What if they mock you?

Pronomus: Then I'll stand by the door....

Chremes: And?

Pronomus: I'll snatch food from the trays as they go by.

Chremes: Then I'll see you at the feast. I'm going to get my

property ready to give to our new leader.

Pronomus: I'll help you carry it.

Chremes: O no you won't. I wouldn't be surprised if you told

the Princess-President that I was helping you deliver

your share. (Exit Chremes).

Pronomus: By the Gods, I need a good plan to keep my own

property, and get a share of everyone elses. That's

what I call justice. I'll think of something on my way

to the feast. (Exit Pronomus).

(Enter 1st Hag).

1st Hag: Where in the world are all the men? I've been

waiting and waiting, stylishly dressed and painted,

ready to sing in my splendid voice, displaying myself

sensuously to snare a man, if one goes by. O spirit of

the Muses, enter into me with a voluptuous song.

(Sings). O Godess of Love, send me my heart's desire!

(Enter Girl).

Girl:

You ugly old hag, did you think you could wait here and trap an unsuspecting man. I'll sing my own song, and let the audience decide which is sweeter. (Sings). O Goddess of Love, send me my hearts desire! (An ugly old man crosses the stage).

1st Hag:

(Pointing to the old man). Call that old man, then sleep with him! But let there be music for my song. (Sings). "If a man wishes to feel a thrill, then he should sleep with me. For what do young girls know of love? A ripe fruit meant for only one mouth at a time, that's me. I give more than any man could ask, and I wouldn't leave him for another like a careless child."

Girl: You envy young women for the pleasure they can

give and take; their tender limbs, soft thighs, sweet

breasts; while you dress and paint yourself like a

corpse.

1st Hag: May your teeth fall out, and your bed collapse with

your lovers' weight and crack your head on the floor.

May your lovers' stiff snake never come awake, not

even with your pleading kisses.

Girl: (Sings). Alas! Alas! Whatever shall I do? My lover has

not come and I am all alone. (End song). My mother

has gone out. But I must ignore this filthy hag.

Where's my nurse? May she bring my lover to me, so

that we may take pleasure.

1st Hag: You wretched slut, you'd better become a lesbian. At

least you might get someone. But I'll get the man of

my choice.

Girl: Croak as much as you like, and peep out of your hole

                 like a weasel. No one will prefer you to me.

1st Hag: May your song choke you.

Girl: Many men will come to you... For your funeral.

1st Hag: They won't!

Girl: Foolish old hag!

1st Hag: Let's not discuss my age.

Girl: Then take off some of your make-up, so we can tell if

                 you're alive or dead.

1st Hag: Why do you abuse me?

Girl: Why do you lay in wait for my lover?

1st Hag: Me? I'm only singing a song in honor of a fine young

                 man.

Girl: You should stay with dirty old men.

1st Hag: I like young men.... Look. There he is.

Girl: He won't want an old, diseased hag.

1st Hag: He won't want a skinny, useless stick.

Girl: He'll pick the one he wants. (Exit Girl).

1st Hag: I'll go too, and let him make his choice.

(Exit Hag. Enter Epigenes).

Epigenes: If only it was permissible to sleep with a beautiful

                   girl, without having to first sleep with an ugly old

                   hag. The new laws are intolerable to a free man.

1st Hag: (Peeking out and talking aside to the audience). By

                   the Gods, you'll pay for chasing young girls. These

                   are no longer the old days of free choice. Everyone

                   must obey the law in a democratic society. But I'll

                   hide here to see what he does. (Exits).

Epigenes: O heavenly gods, may I find my beautiful love alone.

                   For I am drunk with wine and desire.

Girl: (Cautiously peeping out). I fooled that cursed old

                   woman. She left, thinking that I would stay indoors.

1st Hag: (Peeping out). It's he! The man I've been yearning for. (Sings). Come to me, my beloved, come to me. Join me in my bed tonight, where I can run my hands through your precious curls, that stir the fires of my lust, and leave me limp. Help me, Goddess of Love, I implore you. Put him in my arms tonight.

Epigenes: (Sings). Come to me. Come to me. Rush to the door and let me in, or I will fall upon your doorstep in despair. Come, my beloved. Let me rest on your sweet breast. O Aphrodite, you've made me mad with lust. Help me, goddess of love, put her in my arms tonight. But I have sung my woe enough. O my beloved, I beseech you, open the door to my embrace. Your denial makes me ache the more for you, most precious golden object. Daughter of Aphrodite, honeybee of the Muses, suckling of the

Graces, face of the Enchantress, let me in. Embrace

me. I suffer love's pains for you.

1st Hag: (Enters quickly). Who's that knocking at my door? Do

you want me?

Epigenes: Definitely not!

1st Hag: But you were knocking wildly at my door.

Epigenes: May I perish if I did.

1st Hag: Then who were you singing that song for?

Epigenes: A certain young man of my acquaintance.

1st Hag: What's his name?

Epigenes: No one you know.

1st Hag: (Seizing him by the arm). I know you, by Aphrodite!

And I will have you, whether you like it or not.

Epigenes: We're not dealing with senior citizen problems right

now. They've been postponed 'til tomorrow. We're

only handling youngsters under twenty today.

1st Hag: That was allowed by the old government, you

                handsome piece of flesh. But now the law says that

                mature women are first.

Epigenes: Yes, for someone who desires you. But I don't have

                to follow that rule if I'm not hungry.

1st Hag: Did you dine according to the rules?

Epigenes: I don't know what you mean. I must knock at this

                door.

1st Hag: Only after you have knocked at my door.

Epigenes: I don't want a sack of moldy oats.

1st Hag: I know that I'm loved. But you're surprised to find a

                beautiful woman out alone. Press your lips to mine.

Epigenes: No, dear lady. I'm afraid of your lover.

1st Hag: Who?

Epigenes: That great painter.

1st Hag: Who is that?

Epigenes: The painter of the funeral urns. Go inside! So he

               doesn't see your corpse at the door.

1st Hag: I know what you want.

Epigenes: by Zeus, I know what you want!

1st Hag: By Aphrodite, who I serve faithfully, I will not let you

               go.

Epigenes: You are mad, old crone.

1st Hag: You're raving foolishly, for I will take you to my bed.

Epigenes: When we let a bucket down into the well, we'll use

               your hands for hooks, to bring it up again.

1st Hag: Do not insult me, you wretch, but come with me to

               my house.

Epigenes: I don't have to, unless you paid the state tax for each

               one of your considerable years.

1st Hag: By Aphrodite, you must! For nothing excites me

               more than sleeping with a young man.

Epigenes: Nothing makes me feel worse than sleeping with an

                 old hag. I won't do it.

1st Hag: (Takes out decree). By Zeus, this will make you obey.

Epigenes: What is it?

1st Hag: An official decree, which says you must come with

                 me.

Epigenes: Read it, whatever it may be.

1st Hag: Listen carefully, while I read. (Reads). The women in

                 Assembly have decreed that if a young man desires a

                 young woman, he may not sleep with her until he

                 first sleeps with an old woman. But if he isn't willing

                 to sleep with the old woman first, and tries to get the

                 young woman, the new law allows the old woman to

                 carry him off and do whatever she wants to him.

Epigenes: Woe is me! What am I to do?

1st Hag: You must obey the law.

Epigenes: What if a relative or friend wants to rescue me, and

will pay you to let me go?

1st Hag: Men can no longer pay with promises. Only women

can do business now.

Epigenes: Perhaps we can reach an agreement?

1st Hag: No. No bargaining allowed.

Epigenes: I could pretend to be a merchant.

1st Hag: No, you won't. You'd be punished.

Epigenes: What must I do?

1st Hag: Follow me to my house.

Epigenes: Why do I have to do this?

1st Hag: It's necessary to please the new authorities.

Epigenes: Then prepare my funeral bed, for I shall surely die.

1st Hag: (Sarcastically). Surely you'll buy flowers for me first!

Epigenes: Yes, by Zeus. I'll cover your corpse with falling petals.

Girl: (Quickly enters from house). Where are you taking

this man?

1st Hag: I'm taking him home.

Girl: You're being indiscreet, for he's much too young to

              sleep with you. You should be his mother, rather

              than his lover. If you insist on obeying this law,

              there'll be an Oedipus in every bed.

1st Hag: You abominable wretch. You thought of this

              argument out of envy, to embarrass me. But I'll have

              my revenge. (Exit).

Epigenes: By Zeus the preserver, you saved me from a horrible

              hag, my darling. Therefore, to reward you for your

              gallant rescue, tonight I will thank you at great

              length. (Girl takes him by the arm to lead him

              indoors).

2nd Hag: (Enters suddenly). Stop, you! Where do you think

              you're taking this man? You are violating the law,

              which says that he must sleep with me first.

Epigenes: Alas, what misery! Where did you come from, you
                 curse from the underworld? This hag is uglier than
                 the first one.

2nd Hag: (Trying to carry him off). Come with me!

Epigenes: (to the girl). Don't let me be carried off by this
                 abominable old woman. I implore you.

2nd Hag: I'm not carrying you off. It's the law that's carrying
                 you off. (Exit Girl).

Epigenes: It's not the law carrying me off, but Medusa, turning
                 my heart to stone.

2nd Hag: Follow me this way, quickly, my darling, and don't
                 whine!

Epigenes: O, let me find a toilet and ease my bladder, and
                 recover my self control, otherwise you'll see me
                 leaving yellow stains on this spot from fear and
                 shame.

| 2nd Hag: | Be brave! Come along! You can relieve yourself in my house. |

2nd Hag: Be brave! Come along! You can relieve yourself in my

house.

Epigenes: I'm afraid that I'll burst. I'll find a place and be back

right away. I guarantee that.

2nd Hag: No guarantees for me.

3rd Hag: (Enter 3rd hag, running up). Wherever are you going

with her?

Epigenes: I'm not going, I'm being kidnapped. But may the gods

bless you, whoever you may be, for rescuing me

from a horrible fate. (Sees the 3rd Hag). O you

immortal gods! O you demons! O you terrors of the

night! This monstrosity is more dreadful than the

other one. What are you? I implore you to tell me.

Have you risen from the dead?

3rd Hag: Do not insult me, but come with me.

2nd Hag: O, no. You're coming with me.

3rd Hag: You can be sure that I'll never let you go.

2nd Hag: Neither will I.

Epigenes: May the gods curse you, you'll tear me in half.

2nd Hag: You must obey the law and come with me.

3rd Hag: Not if an older and uglier woman appears.

Epigenes: If I perish first with you, how shall I ever get to see a

               beautiful young woman.

3rd Hag: That's your problem, but obey you must.

Epigenes: Then I must sleep with one of you first, in order to

               get free?

2nd Hag: Don't you know? You must come with me.

Epigenes: Then tell this one to let me go.

3rd Hag: O, no. You must come with me.

Epigenes: Certainly. If she'll let me go.

2nd Hag: I won't, by Zeus.

3rd Hag: Neither will I.

Epigenes: You would be dangerous on a ferryboat.

2nd Hag: Why?

Epigenes: You'd tear the passengers in half, before setting

                 them ashore.

2nd Hag: Shut up! And follow me.

3rd Hag: By Zeus, no. You're going with me.

Epigenes: This situation is what the law meant. I must sleep

                 with both of these old boats. But how do I row them

                 at the same time?

2nd Hag: Eat something nutritious and you'll do fine.

Epigenes: Woe is me! They've just about carried me off. (2nd

                 and 3rd Hag struggle for Epigenes, dragging him back

                 and forth).

3rd Hag: (to 2nd Hag). You won't get anything, for I'll go

                 wherever you do.

Epigenes: By the gods, don't let her! It's better to endure one

                 affliction, then both.

3rd Hag: Both it will be! Whether you like it or not.

Epigenes: I am twice cursed if I must first sleep with an ugly,

old hag, and as soon as I am finished with her, have

to service another hag, older and uglier than the

first. Am I not the most wretched of mortals? By Zeus

the preserver, an unhappy man, unfortunate enough

to be preyed on by two wild beasts. Nevertheless, if I

perish from exposure to these brutes, bury me head

first at the entrance to one hag, and feet towards the

entrance of the other. Then let them be covered with

clay, and bake them until they become funeral urns.

They shall be a memorial to a lost youth. (The Hags

pull him out. Exit).

(Enter Maidservant).

Maidservant: O happy people, and happy me, and my mistress

who who is happiest of all. All you happy citizens at

our door, our happy neighbors, all our fellow

townsmen, and I, the happiest of servant girls, who

have anointed myself with precious oils, by Zeus!

And the fine wine that I have drunk. It's the best

thing in the world! By the Gods, it makes a woman

feel warm and passionate all night. But tell me, kind

women, where is my master? That is, the husband of

my mistress.

Chorus: We think you'll find him if you wait here.

Maidservant: You're right. Here he comes, probably rushing to get

to the feast! (Enter Blepyros). Master, master, o

happy, thrice blessed master!

Blepyros: Me?

Maidservant: Yes, you, by Zeus, as no man ever was. For who could

be happier than you, who has not yet eaten at the

feast. You alone in the whole city who has not dined.

Blepyros: You're certainly describing a happy man.

Maidservant: Where are you going?

Blepyros: I'm going to the feast.

Maidservant: By Aphrodite, last again. Nevertheless, your wife ordered me to find you and look after you. And she told me that if our audience enjoyed the show, let them also come to the feast. So invite them all, for the feast is for everyone. There is plenty of wine to drink and delicious morsels to be gobbled down. So don't waste any more time, and let the audience come along too. There's enough for everybody!

Blepyros: Let everyone join us. Invite them all. And while you are preparing to go, beautiful maidens will dance for you. But first, a serious word with you. If you enjoyed our cleverness and jokes, and our beauty, remember to judge us justly and let us know. But now it's time to go.

(Exit Choral dance).

THE AVENUE OF THE
AMERICAS
ASSOCIATION'S
CONCERTS IN THE PARK

The Birds

(Enter Euelpides, Pisthetairus, Servant carrying birds).

Euelpides:	(to his Jackdaw). Do you want me to walk into someone.
Pisthetairus:	Damn you! This dumb bird keeps croaking: "turn back."
Euelpides:	(to his bird). You villain! Why are we wandering around like this? We'll perish from going up and down this road without a destination.
Pisthetairus:	What misery! I listened to an old crow and now we're lost!
Euelpides:	I've worn off my toe-nails obeying a Jackdaw!
Pisthetairus:	I have no idea where we are.
Euelpides:	Could you find your way home again?

Pisthetairus: By Zeus! No one could find their way home from here.

Euelpides: Woe is me.

Pisthetairus: We're lost. Lost.

Euelpides: The birdseller treated us badly. The lunatic swore that these birds would lead us to Tereus the Hoopoe, the man who became a bird. Instead, all they do is bite and complain. (To the Jackdaw). What are you gaping at? We've lost our way.

Pisthetairus: You're right, by Zeus! I don't see a path.

Euelpides: Does that wretched bird have anything to say?

Pisthetairus: He's croaking a different tune now.

Euelpides: Where does he say we should go?

Pisthetairus: He says he'll bite my fingers off.

Euelpides: Isn't it strange that when all we wish is to peacefully visit the birds, we can't find the way? (To the audience). For know, my friends, that we're suffering from a different disease than that infecting

foreigners who are eager to become citizens of our

country. We had a place of honor and flew away

without anyone chasing us; not because we hate our

land, for Athens is a great and prosperous place,

where everyone wastes their wealth on lawsuits. A

grasshopper briefly sings his song in the fields, while

a citizen sings his life away in the lawcourts. That's

why we're wandering along, searching for a quiet

place to settle down. We want to find Tereus, the

Hoopoe, and ask him if he knows the right city for us.

Pisthetairus: Hey!

Euelpides: What?

Pisthetairus: My crow keeps pointing up.

Euelpides: So does this one.... He's trying to show me

something. There must be birds nearby. We'll find

out if we make noise.

Pisthetairus: Do you know what to do? Kick something.

Euelpides: Knock your head against something.

Pisthetairus: Then make some kind of loud noise.

Euelpides: Allright. (Makes a loud noise). Here birdie. Here

birdie.

Pisthetairus: What are you doing? You can't call the King of the

birds like that. You should call Hoopoe, Hoopoe.

Euelpides: Hoopoe, Hoopoe. How long do I have to call Hoopoe,

Hoopoe?

Trochilus: (offstage). Who is that? (Enters). Who is yelling for

my master?

Euelpides: Apollo preserve us! What a snout! (Exit Servant with

birds).

Trochilus: Alas! These are men! Birdhunters!

Euelpides: Don't be alarmed. You have nothing to fear from us.

Trochilus: You shall be put to death!

Euelpides: But we're not men.

Trochilus: What are you?

Euelpides: I'm a yellow-billed crapper bird.

Trochilus: You're babbling nonsense.

Euelpides: Wait and see what drops between my legs.

Trochilus: (to Pisthetairus). What kind of bird are you?....

                  Speak!

Pisthetairus: I'm an ashen-face trembler bird from overseas.

Euelpides: What kind of creature are you?

Trochilus: I'm a slave bird.

Euelpides: Were you captured in a bird battle?

Trochilus: No. When my master became a Hoopoe he asked me

                  to become a bird, so I could continue to serve him.

Euelpides: Does a bird need a servant?

Trochilus: Certainly! He was a man once and sometimes he still

                  yearns for anchovies. Then I take a dish and fly off to

                  get them. Or if he wants pea-soup, I fetch the pot

                  and ladle.

Euelpides:	Then you're a fetching bird. Hurry inside and fetch your master.
Trochilus:	I can't, by Zeus! He's napping after a delicious feast of bugs and berries.
Euelpides:	Then wake him.
Trochilus:	He'll be furious…. But I'll wake him. (Exit).
Pisthetairus:	(looking after Trochilus). May you perish miserably, for almost frightening me to death.
Euelpides:	Woe is me! Even my Jackdaw was scared away.
Pisthetairus:	You cowardly beast. You were so scared you let our birds get away.
Euelpides:	Didn't your crow get away while you were cowering in fear?
Pisthetairus:	Not me, by Zeus!
Euelpides:	Where is he?
Pisthetairus:	He flew away.

Euelpides: And you didn't let him go! How brave you are,

honorable sir.

Epops: (offstage). Open the forest, so I may enter! (Enter

Epops).

Euelpides: By Heracles! What a strange beast! What plumage!

What a crest!

Epops: Who seeks me?

Euelpides: The Olympian gods have played a dirty trick on you.

Epops: Are you laughing at my plumage? Don't you dare,

strangers, for I was once a man!

Euelpides: We're not laughing at you .

Epops: What then?

Euelpides: Your beak looks ridiculous to us.

Epops: This is how Sophocles describes me in his plays.

Euelpides: Then you are Tereus? The man who became a bird?

We didn't know who you were.

Epops: I'm a bird.

Euelpides: Where are your feathers?

Epops: They've fallen off.

Euelpides: From a disease?

Epops: No. During the winter all birds moult. Then they grow

               new feathers in spring. But tell me who you are.

Euelpides: We are men.

Epops: From what country?

Euelpides: From Athens, the land of beautiful ships.

Epops: Are you lawyers?

Euelpides: No sir! We detest lawyers.

Epops: You must be unusual men.

Euelpides: There are others, though they're hard to find.

Epops: But why have you come here?

Euelpides: We want advice.

Epops: About what?

Euelpides: First, because you were once a man like us; and once

               owed money, like us; and once enjoyed not paying,

just like us. Second, since you became a bird, you
have flown over land and sea and know as much as
man and bird can know. That's why we've come to
you as suppliants, for you to tell us of a noble city
where we can nest.

Epops: A nobler city than your own?

Euelpides: Not nobler, but less demanding.

Epops: Do you want an aristocratic government?

Euelpides: Not me! I hate tyranny!

Epops: What kind of city do you want?

Euelpides: One where the most important business would be a
friend, coming to my door early in the morning,
saying: "By the Olympic Zeus. Join me soon, after you
have washed your children, for I am about to give a
marriage feast. And if you won't visit me when I'm
prosperous, don't join me when I'm poor."

Epops: By Zeus, you prefer times of plenty. (To Pisthetairus).

                What about you?

Pisthetairus: I'm also fond of such things.

Epops: What things?

Pisthetairus: Where the father of a handsome boy complains

                when he meets me, as if I'd insulted him: "You were

                very rude when you met my son returning from the

                Gymnasium, after his bath, and didn't say hello, and

                take his hand, or kiss him, although you are my good

                friend."

Epops: You poor fellow. What hardships you long for! I know

                a city for you on the Red Sea.

Euelpides: Nothing by the sea; for one morning a ship will sail in

                bringing a summons to appear in court. Do you know

                a Greek city?

Epops: Why not go and live in Lepreum?

Euelpides: No lepers. No leprosy. No Lepreum.

Epops: What about the city of the one-eyed Locrians?

Euelpides: Not for a pile of gold. Someplace with two eyes. But

                what about life among the birds? You should know

                about that.

Epops: Not an unpleasant place to live. First you must throw

                away your purse.

Euelpides: That would remove most of man's dishonesty.

Epops: Then you dine in gardens, on sesame seeds, myrtle

                berries, poppy seeds and mint.

Euelpides: (to Pisthetairus). That sounds like a healthy feast.

Pisthetairus: (awakening out of a profound reverie). Hah! Hah!

                Truly I have a great plan that will give power to the

                birds, if you'll just obey me.

Epops: How shall we obey you?

Pisthetairus: How shall you obey me? To begin with: don't fly

                around with open beaks. It's too undignified. And

                don't flutter! Men despise flutterers. They say birds

are more unstable than humans: fluttering,

inconsistent and never roosting in the same place

twice.

Epops: By Dionysus, you're right! What should we do?

Pisthetairus: Build a city in the sky!

Epops: What sort of city could we birds build?

Pisthetairus: Now really. What a stupid thing to say. Look down.

Epops: Well, I'm looking.

Pisthetairus: Now look up.

Epops: I am looking up.

Pisthetairus: Turn your head around.

Epops: By Zeus, I'll get a twisted neck.

Pisthetairus: Did you see anything?

Epops: Yes, the clouds and the heavens.

Pisthetairus: Don't you see the astronomical pole of the birds?

Epops: What pole?

Pisthetairus: The pole that rotates and revolves everywhere.
That's why it's called a pole. If you build a city in the
atmosphere, it will be called a Polis. If you fortify the
Polis and rule men as if they were insects, it will be
called a metropolis. On the other hand, you can rule
the gods by starving them.

Epops: How?

Pisthetairus: Your atmosphere is midway between heaven and
earth. Just as pilgrims ask for safe passage to a holy
place; when men burn offerings to the gods, if the
gods won't pay tribute to the birds, you won't allow
the sweet smoke of the offerings to pass safely
through your metropolis and reach the gods.

Epops: Aha! Aha! By all the snares and traps of man! What a
clever plan! I'll build the city with you, if the other
birds agree.

Pisthetairus: Who will explain the plan to them?

Epops: You will. I've taught them human speech, instead of
                their barbarian talk.

Pisthetairus: How will we tell all of them?

Epops: Easily. I shall wake my wife, the nightingale, and she
                and I shall sing a song to summon the birds.

Pisthetairus: O finest of birds, quickly wake your wife, the
                nightingale.

Epops: (song). Dearest wife, awake from slumber, raise your
                voice in heavenly song. Let the sweet notes flow
                from your pure throat in sad lament for our lost son,
                Itys. Itys. Your song will rise to Zeus above, where
                golden-haired Apollo, stirred to beauty by your tune,
                will lead a chorus of immortal gods in blessed song.

Pisthetairus: By Zeus! The bird has a splendid voice! What a fine
                song!

Euelpides: Shhh!

Pisthetairus: What's the matter?

Euelpides: Be quiet!

Pisthetairus: Why?

Euelpides: The Epops wants to sing again.

Epops: (song). Epopopopopopopopopoi! Lo! Lo! Come,

come come, come, come, come forth, my fellow

birds. Flocks from fields and forests swiftly fly here.

Tio, tio, tio, tio, tio,tio! Mountain birds and garden

birds, answer my call! Trioto, trioto, totobrix! Birds

from swamp and seashore, from the sweet nesting

places of the earth, long neck and short beaks, speed

across the hallowed plains of Marathon. For a

cunning old man has come here with new ideas, a

clever plan for a daring venture for the birds. Come

hither to a conference, one and all!

Torotorotorotorotix! Ciccabu, ciccabu!

Torotorotorotorolililix.

Pisthetairus: Do you see any birds?

Euelpides: By Apollo, not one! No matter where I look.

Pisthetairus: It seems that all that clucking was useless. (Enter

                  Flamingo).

Flamingo: Torotix, torotix!

Pisthetairus: Look, my dear sir. There's a bird!

Euelpides: By Zeus, you're right! What kind is it? Is it a Peacock?

Pisthetairus: Epops will tell us. What kind of bird is this?

Epops: This is not a common, ordinary bird that you see all

                  the time; it's a water-fowl.

Pisthetairus: Beautiful…. And flaming red!

Epops: That's close, for it's a flamingo.

Euelpides: (enter bird of Paradise). Look! Look!

Pisthetairus: What is it?

Euelpides: There's another bird!

Pisthetairus: By Zeus, it is. What kind is it?

Epops: It's the bird of Paradise. (Enter 2nd Hoopoe).

Euelpides: Here comes another, with a crest! It's another

                  Hoopoe.

Pisthetairus: What a strange creature.

Epops: This is my grandchild.

Pisthetairus: He's lost a lot of feathers!

Epops: Yes. He's a rich and famous bird, so scheming

                  lawyers and designing females have almost plucked

                  him bald. (Enter Pelican).

Pisthetairus: By Poseidon! Who is this?

Epops: This is the glutton.

Pisthetairus: We all know him.

Euelpides: We see him everywhere. (Enter the remaining birds

                  of the chorus, traditionally totaling 24).

Pisthetairus: By Poseidon! What a plague of birds!

Euelpides: By Apollo! They fill the air. I can hardly see anything

                  through their fluttering.

Pisthetairus: Here's a Partridge! There's a duck, by Zeus! And

there's a Kingfisher! (The traditional entrance of the

Chorus formed into the Hemichoria – 12 males on

one side, 12 females on the other).

Euelpides: There's an owl!

Pisthetairus: A jay, a dove, lark, buzzard, pigeon, heron, falcon,

cuckoo, osprey, woodpecker.

Euelpides: Oh! Oh! The birds! The black birds! See them twitter

and chirp and hop about! Are they threatening us?

Oh my! Their beaks are gaping wide, menacing you

and me.

Pisthetairus: You're right.

Chorus: Popopopopopopi! Who called us?

Epops: I did! Loyally serving my friends.

Chorus: Tifitifitifitifitifitifi! What news do you have?

Epops: Something reasonable, pleasant, safe and profitable,

for two clever visitors have arrived.

Chorus: Who? Where? How? Why?

Epops: Know my friends, that two wise men have come

              from Athens with an incredible plan.

Chorus: You've committed the greatest crime since I was a

              nestling! How could you?

Epops: Don't be afraid to listen.

Chorus: What have you done?

Epops: I've welcomed humans who admire our society.

Chorus: Have you really done this?

Epops: Yes. And I'm delighted that they're here.

Chorus: Are they nearby?

Epops: As near as I am.

Chorus: Woe! Woe! Betrayed! We've suffered a horrible fate!

              For you who were our friend and fed in fields at our

              side, have broken the ancient laws and have violated

              the oath of the birds. You summoned us here to

              deceive us and exposed us to a shameful race. The

race of man, which has always been the enemy of the birds. As for you, we'll judge you later. I propose we punish these humans now, by pecking them to pieces.

Pisthetairus: Alas, we're doomed!

Euelpides: It's all your fault. Why did you bring me here?

Pisthetairus: To be together.

Euelpides: So I could weep my last tears?

Pisthetairus: Don't quibble about tears, for how could you weep once your eyes were pecked out?

Chorus: Ho! Ho! Attack. Lead a hostile, deadly charge. Spread wide your wings. Surround them, for both of them will howl in pain and be devoured by hungry beaks. Neither is there a snow-capped mountain, nor fleecy cloud, nor foamy sea, where these mortal foes shall flee to escape us. Let us delay no longer, but attack with beak and claw. Where is the war leader of the

birds? Let him lead a charge on the right flank.

Euelpides: This is the end! Where shall I fly, unhappy man?

Pisthetairus: Stop! Stay here.

Euelpides: So they can tear us apart?

Pisthetairus: How do you think you'll escape them?

Euelpides: I don't know.

Pisthetairus: Then I'll tell you. We must remain here and fight for

our lives.

Euelpides: Against the beaks and claws of these fierce birds?

Pisthetairus: Prepare to defend yourself.

Euelpides: What about our eyes?

Pisthetairus: Protect them with one arm.

Euelpides: O cleverest of men, preparing me for battle with a

general's clever strategy.

Chorus: Eleleleu! Present beaks! Advance! Don't wait any

longer! Tear, pluck, strike, scratch, peck their eyes

first!

Epops: Stop! O vilest of all ferocious beasts! Why are you

trying to tear to pieces and destroy these humans,

who are related to my wife, and who haven't harmed

you?

Chorus: If we spare men who are crueler than wolves, we

wouldn't be able to punish anyone.

Epops: They may be enemies by nature, but they're friends

in spirit. They've come to teach you something

important.

Chorus: How could these enemies of our ancestors teach us

anything useful?

Epops: Surely the wise can learn much from their enemies,

for caution can mean your salvation. You'd never

learn this from a friend, but your enemy forces you

to learn it. For instance, nations learned to build strong defenses and warships from enemies, not friends. This lesson preserves children, homes and possessions.

Chorus: It seems to me it might be useful to listen to them first, for we could even learn something from our enemies.

Pisthetairus: They're not as furious as they were before. Move back.

Epops: It's the right thing too. You should do it for me as a favor.

Chorus: Well, truthfully, we've never opposed you in anything.

Pisthetairus: They are definitely calmer. So lower your arms and walk around, but be ready to defend yourself, for we can't run away.

Euelpides: Agreed. But if we are killed, where shall we be

buried?

Pisthetairus: In the public cemetery. We shall have a noble funeral

when Athens learns that we died in glorious battle,

fighting a dreadful enemy.

Chorus: Move back a ways. Sheath your fury and your claws!

Let's ask these travelers who they are, where they're

from and why they're here. Ho! Epops!

Epops: What do you want?

Chorus: Who are these mortals, and where are they from?

Epops: Strangers from learned Greece.

Chorus: What brings them to the birds?

Epops: They admire you and your way of life, and wish to

live among you.

Chorus: What are you telling us? What do they say?

Epops: Incredible and wondrous things.

Chorus: Why is it to their advantage to live with us? Will they

learn from us how to defeat their foes or help their

friends?

Epops: One of them describes tremendous happiness

beyond belief. He will convince you that the birds

should rule everything.

Chorus: Is he mad?

Epops: He's very sensible.

Chorus: Is he at all wise?

Epops: A cunning fox, a sly rogue, a tricky rascal, but a

clever, subtle fellow.

Chorus: Order him to speak! Let him tell us his scheme! If

what you say is true, I can't wait to hear him.

Epops: In the name of the gods, tell everyone what I

summoned them to hear.

Pisthetairus: Not I, by Apollo! Not unless everyone agrees that

there'll be no more scratching or pecking.

Chorus: You don't mean pecking the _______? By no means!

Pisthetairus: I meant the eyes.

Chorus: We agree then.

Pisthetairus: Swear to it.

Chorus: We swear not to harm you, as we hope to please our

audience.

Pisthetairus: So be it.

Chorus: But if we break our word, may the audience detest

us.

Pisthetairus: Agreed! Agreed! Let the warrior birds go home, and

we'll send them news about our talk. (Exit some

birds).

Chorus: Mankind is naturally deceitful in every way! But we

shall listen to you. Perhaps you might mention

something good about us, or notice some great gift

or talent that we neglected, but you discovered.

Speak for the public good: whatever good you do will

benefit all the birds. So be assured we will not harm

you first and boldly tell us why you're here.

Pisthetairus: Well, by Zeus, I'm eager to begin, but in the threat of

battle I forgot the speech I had prepared. Bring

napkins and water so I can wash my hands.

Euelpides: Are we having a feast?

Pisthetairus: No, by Zeus, but I've been looking for a gigantic

behemoth of a word that would enter the minds of

these poor birds. O so much do I sympathize with

them, who were once kings….

Chorus: Kings? We were kings? Kings of what?

Pisthetairus: Of everything that exists. Of me, you, Zeus himself,

the ancient gods, Cronus and the Titans, and the

earth.

Chorus: The earth?

Pisthetairus: Yes, by Apollo.

Chorus: By Zeus, we didn't know this.

Pisthetairus: That's because you are uneducated and ignorant of

Philosophy. You don't even read Aesop's Fables,

where the lark was the first creation, before the

earth. And when her father died of a terrible illness,

there was no earth to bury him in! So he lay there for

five days and the lark didn't know what to do, so she

buried him in her own head.

Euelpides: Then he's underneath a headstone now.

Epops: Isn't the rulership of everything rightly theirs, if they

existed before the earth and gods, and are the

oldest?

Euelpides: Certainly, by Apollo! Therefore sharpen your beaks,

for Zeus and the gods won't vacate their thrones for

a woodpecker.

Pisthetairus: There are many proofs of this. For in ancient times,

not the gods, but the birds were rulers and kings

over men. For example, consider the rooster, who

was the sovereign ruler of the Persians, before

Darius and Xerxes. He is still called the Persian bird

from that time.

Euelpides: Since this tale then, he alone struts around with his

crest erect upon his head, like a great king.

Pisthetairus: So powerful was he, so mighty then, that even today,

with only the memory of his power, when he merely

crows at dawn, everyone jumps out of bed and

rushes to work: bakers, farmers, soldiers, laborers;

all get dressed and trudge off.

Euelpides: I know that's true, for he cost me a wool cloak. Once

I was invited to an early morning celebration. I went

to bed the night before and just fell asleep when the

rooster crowed. I got dressed, rushed out into the

night and on my way to my friend's house a robber

stole my cloak.

Pisthetairus: At the same time, the kite was ruler and king of the

Greeks.

Epops: Of the Greeks?

Pisthetairus: When he was king, he was the first to teach the

Greeks to bow down to the ground before the kites.

Euelpides: Yes, by Dionysus! I was going home once and saw a

kite, fell down, rolled on my back, and swallowed all

my money.

Pisthetairus: A cuckoo was king of Egypt and Phoenicia, and when

he cried: "cuckoo", all his subjects ran into the fields

to cut their wheat and barley.

Euelpides: They went cuckoo, then.

Pisthetairus: The birds' power was so great that when a man was

king, an Agamemnon or Menelaus, a bird sat upon

their scepters, sharing all the bribes they received.

Euelpides: I didn't know that. And I always wondered why a

great leader would always appear with a bird of

state. Now I see that the bird was supposed to watch what bribes the leader took.

Pisthetairus: What is most remarkable is that Zeus, king of the gods, stands with an eagle on his head, because he is a king. His daughter, Athene, has an owl. His son, Apollo, has a hawk.

Euelpides: By the goddesses, you describe them well. Why do they have birds?

Pisthetairus: So when man offered sacrifices to the gods, the birds could get their share first. And no man would swear by the gods on those days, but by the birds. To this very day, people swear by the birds when they're deceiving each other. Once, long ago, man thought that you were great and powerful, now they think you're slaves, fools, worthless. They throw rocks at you, as if you were mad. Birdhunters catch you in snares, traps, nets and sacks, and stuff you in tiny cages and sell you. Shoppers come to the market and squeeze you, poke you and buy you. After they handle you, they take you home and cook you. They don't merely roast you. They cover you with oil, grated cheese, spices, wine and other ingredients, and serve you with sauce, as if you had no natural flavor of your own.

Chorus: Alas! Alas! O mortal, you've brought such sad reminders of the past. I detest the worthlessness of our fathers, who wasted their fathers' power and lost it all, to our greatest harm! But surely the gods have sent you to us to be our savior. For we'll dwell in safety if we entrust our lives and children to you. Now that you're here, tell us what to do. Life is no longer worth living if we don't do everything we can to recover our lost kingdom.

Pisthetairus: Well now, first I advise you to live together in one

                  city, for all the birds. Then build a great wall between

                  earth and heaven.

Epops: By the gods! What a powerful city!

Pisthetairus: After the wall is built, you must ask Zeus to restore

                  the ancient kingdom of the birds. If he's unwilling,

                  and refuses, and won't immediately confess that he's

                  wrong, you'll declare war on him. Next, you'll forbid

                  the gods to pass through your kingdom, when

                  they're lustfully going to earth to seduce and ravish

                  mortals. And if they disobey, you'll prevent them

                  from satisfying their desires by making mortals wear

                  chastity belts. Then you'll send an ambassador bird

                  to earth, instructing men to offer sacrifices to the

                  birds, since they are the new rulers. After this, send a

                  bird ambassador to the gods, and assign a special

                  bird to each god, to supervise the sacrifices offered

to the gods. So when there's a sacrifice to the

goddess of love, a lovebird will share the feast, a

seagull will share sacrifices to the seagod, and when

an offering is made to the king of the gods, a

kingfisher will be in charge.

Euelpides: Let mighty Zeus thunder about that!

Epops: Why will men think we're as powerful as the gods,

and not just birds who have wings and fly?

Pisthetairus: You're babbling nonsense. Many of the gods use

wings when they fly. Eros, god of love, flies down and

shoots winged arrows at lovers.

Epops: Won't Zeus get angry and hurl a winged thunder-

bolt at us?

Pisthetairus: If men are too ignorant to recognize your power, and

think the gods in Olympus are rulers, then send a

cloud of sparrows to eat all the seeds in the fields, so

nothing grows. When they get hungry, they'll see
how much the gods help them.

Euelpides: The gods won't do anything but make excuses.

Pisthetairus: For further proof, let the crows peck out the eyes of
their cattle and sheep, then let the gods cure them,
since they claim to help man.

Euelpides: Don't do your test until I sell my sheep!

Pisthetairus: If they acknowledge you as gods, many blessings will
be theirs.

Epops: Tell me about one of them.

Pisthetairus: First, the locusts will never destroy their crops again,
for a flock of owls will eat them, and thrushes will eat
the ants and flies.

Epops: But how shall we give them money? For that's what
they want more than anything.

Pisthetairus: The birds will help miners find precious metals, and
guide sea-faring merchants so they avoid disasters.

Epops: How will they avoid disasters?

Pisthetairus: A bird will always guide them during their voyage,

and warn them about storms and other dangers, and

lead them to profit.

Euelpides: I'll get a ship and become a merchant, and sail off to

make my fortune.

Pisthetairus: The birds will show men hoards of buried treasure,

hidden by misers, who used to say: "only the birds

know where I buried my treasure."

Euelpides: I'll sell my ship and buy a shovel, and dig up lots of

money.

Epops: How will we give them good health, which is a gift of

the gods?

Pisthetairus: If they're prosperous, then they'll be healthy, true?

You can be certain that everyone feels badly when

they're poor.

Epops: Then how will they grow old? For that's a gift from

the gods. Must they die in childhood?

Pisthetairus: No, by Zeus. You'll add three hundred years to their

lives.

Epops: How?

Pisthetairus: By sharing the secrets of wise birds who know how

to live longer.

Euelpides: Oh my! The birds are more worthy than the gods to

rule over us.

Pisthetairus: Aren't they much better? It's not necessary to build

stone temples for them, adorned with golden doors,

for birds dwell in fields and forests. An olive tree will

be a temple for the noble birds, and we won't have

to go to Delphi or other distant shrines to offer

sacrifices, but we'll stand in a grove of trees, holding

up our hands, and pray to the birds for a share of

good fortune. This will immediately be granted when we offer them some bird seed.

Chorus: O, you who were once the most hateful have become the dearest of men. It would be impossible for me to ever disagree with you again. Inspired by your words, I vow and swear that if you join me in an honest alliance against the gods, we birds will win our power back from them. The birds will do whatever should be done by force. You must prepare the plan and we will depend on you.

Epops: By Zeus, there's no more time to sit around like the audience and doze. We have to do something right away. Welcome to my nest. Who are you?

Pisthetairus: I am Pisthetairus, and this is Euelpides.

Epops: You are both welcome.

Pisthetairus: Thank you.

Epops: Come with me to my nest.

Pisthetairus: Thank you. Lead the way.

Epops: Then follow me.

Pisthetairus: By the gods! Come back here! How can we follow

you, when we can't fly?

Epops: That's no problem.

Pisthetairus: But consider Aesop's fable of the fox, who suffered

disaster when he became partners with an eagle.

Epops: Fear nothing. I know a special herb which, if eaten,

will grow wings for you.

Pisthetairus: Then we shall join you.

Chorus: Hello there! I'm calling you!

Epops: What is it?

Chorus: Fly off with these two, and entertain them properly,

but let the sweet-throated nightingale stay here, and

harmonize with the muses, so we may dance.

Pisthetairus: Consent to this, by Zeus! Bring forth the delicate bird from the flowering grove! Bring her out, by the gods, so we may see the beauteous nightingale.

Epops: If it seems appropriate to you, I will do so. Come here, Procne, and show yourself to our guests (enter Procne).

Pisthetairus: O Zeus on high, how beautiful and delicate a bird! How fair!

Euelpides: I'd like to stroke her feathers.

Pisthetairus: Adorned in white and gold, like an innocent child.

Euelpides: I'd like to kiss her in greeting.

Pisthetairus: Don't be silly. She has a sharp beak.

Euelpides: Well, by Zeus, there should be some way to approach her.

Epops: Let us go.

Pisthetairus: Please lead the way, and may success follow us. (Exit Epops, Pisthetairus, Euelpides).

Chorus: O precious gold and white companion, delicate
nightingale, partner of all my songs, dearest of birds!
You have joined us, bringing us your lovely voice! You
who play the sweet-voiced flute, sound the notes of
spring. Begin the choral hymn. Listen now, mankind,
creature of dark nature, as brief and frail as leaves,
helpless clay figures, shadows, gathering in feeble
tribes, wingless creatures of a day, miserable
mortals, men of foolish dreams, pay attention to us,
the immortals, the always existing, the ethereal, the
ageless, who meditate eternally. When you have
truly heard everything from us about sublime things,
the nature of birds, the origin of gods and rivers,
primal matter and creation, you may tell your leaders
and wise men that you have learned the truth. In the
beginning was Chaos and Night, and dark Force, and
the vast underworld; nor was there earth, or air, or

heaven. First black-winged Night lay a wind-egg in the boundless bosom of Force; and as time flew by, the always desirable Eros hatched, glittering with golden wings on his shimmering back, like the swirling whirl- winds. He mated with winged, nocturnal Chaos, in the endless underworld, hatched the race of birds, and led them forth into the light. Thus the immortal gods did not exist, until Eros hatched all things. But then these great forces mated, heaven and earth were created, and oceans, and immortal gods. Therefore, the birds are the oldest of the gods. There are many proofs that we are the first offspring of Eros. We fly; some of us are lovebirds, and help lovers in their romances, so indeed, all the greatest blessings are from the birds. We foretell the weather and planting time; we warn sailors of storms; we tell when the cold is coming so mankind can prepare warm clothes, then tell when

warm weather is coming, so there's time to buy light

clothing. We give you good omens, so you put our

images on everything, including money. You swear

by us, you hold us in your hands, you're bird-

brained, sing like birds, and nickname everything a

bird. You even name your children after us.

Therefore, if you accept us as gods, you'll be able to

use us as prophets, teachers, inspiration, helpers,

guides, and friends. We won't run away and sit

among the clouds with solemn airs, like Zeus, but

being everywhere, we'll give you, and your children,

and your childrens' children, health, wealth,

happiness, long life, peace, youthfulness, laughter,

dancing and feasting. You'll have so many good

things that you'll soon get tired of them. Muse of the

woods, tio, tio, tio, tio, tio, tio, tiotix, singer of many

songs, from valleys to mountain tops, tio, tio, tio, tiotix, perched upon an ash tree, tio, tio, tio, tio, tiotix, I sing from my sweet throat, the sacred songs of lusty Pan, and watch the stately dances in the mountains, of the mother godess, Cybele. Tototo-totototototootix. Where lovers, like the bees, feed upon the honey of our songs, sighing to our sweet refrain. Tio, tio, tio, tiotix. If anyone in the audience wants to change their way of life, and live happily with the birds, join us. For many things that are disgraceful on earth, forbidden by law, are honorable among the birds. If it is against the law to beat your wife, the honorable custom of birds is to run after her and beat her, and say: "Raise your claws, if you dare." If you run away from home, you can find refuge with us in a nest. If you're a foreigner looking for a place to roost, you can be a rooster. and if you

are uncertain of your place in society, like many of
our audience, and you don't know what's good or
bad, join the birds, for we're allowed to make
mistakes. Then the swans appeared, tio, tio, tio, tio,
tio, tio, tiotix, making music with their beating wings,
in a joyous hymn to Apollo: tio, tio, tio, tiotix, sitting
on the banks of the river Hubris, tio, tio, tio, tiotix,
and the hymn rose through the ethereal clouds, and
man and beast cowered, and a breathless calm
stilled the waves; totototototototototoix. All of
Olympus echoed the song, and the gods were
astonished, and the Graces and Muses sang in reply
to the birds: tio, tio, tio, tiotix. Nothing is better nor
more satisfying than to have wings. For example, if
anyone of you in the audience had wings and got
bored while we recited beautiful poetry, because you
were hungry, you could fly off and eat, and when you

were full, fly back to us again. If somebody

desperately had to piss, you wouldn't have to wet

your pants. You could fly off, piss, relax, and fly right

back. And if you're having an affair, and see the

woman's husband in the audience, you could flap

your wings, fly off, make love to her, fly back and

take your seat again. Wouldn't you give anything to

have wings? Look at some of your leaders, who flew

out of nowhere, and now are crowing over everyone.

(Enter Pisthetairus and Euelpides, as birds).

Pisthetairus: Well, so far, so good. By Zeus, I've never seen a

funnier sight.

Euelpides: What are you laughing at?

Pisthetairus: At your feathers. Do you know what you look like in

those feathers? Like a plucked goose, whitewashed

by a poor housepainter.

Euelpides: And you look like a baldheaded crow.

Pisthetairus: These are insults from the plays of Aeschylus: "Thus

we don't suffer from the hands of others, but from

our own feathers...."

Epops: What should we do now?

Pisthetairus: First we should name our city something great and

illustrious, then we should offer a sacrifice to the

gods.

Euelpides: I think that's proper.

Epops: Now let me see, what shall we name our city?

Pisthetairus: Do you want to call it by that distinguished

Lacedaemonian name, Sparta?

Euelpides: O Heracles! Should I name my own city Sparta? If I

needed a rope to tie my bed together, I wouldn't call

it Sparta!

Pisthetairus: Then what shall we call it?

Euelpides: Something splendid, worthy of the lofty clouds and

elevated spaces.

Pisthetairus: What about 'Cloud-cuckoo-town.'

Epops: Excellent! Excellent! What a magnificent name.

Euelpides: Is this the Cloud-cuckoo-town where people

pretending to be rich always claim to have great

estates?

Pisthetairus: Yes, indeed. It's that wonderful place where the

Olympian gods outbragged their enemies, the Titans.

Euelpides: What a fine city! What god will be the patron

protector of the city? What clothes should we buy

for the god?

Pisthetairus: Why not let Athene be the guardian of the city?

Euelpides: How could a city be well-governed and protected

when a woman is appointed the ruler, without even

being elected? Will the men stay at home and knit?

Pisthetairus: Then who will command our city's army?

Epops: A bird from our own company, the fighting rooster.

Euelpides: A chicken general! Our god will love to live in a

chicken coop!

Pisthetairus: (to Euelpides). Behave now, and fly off and help the

builders. Let them gather rocks, prepare mortar and

carry it to the wall. Climb up and down the ladders,

station guards at their posts, tend the fires, inspect

everything and sleep there, and send two heralds,

one to the gods above, the other to men below, then

report back to me.

Euelpides: Report back! May pestilence take you for all I care!

Pisthetairus: Go ahead, my dear helper, do as I tell you, for none

of my plans can work without you. (Exit Euelpides). I

will summon the priest to lead the procession, so I

may sacrifice to the new gods. Have a servant bring

the offering basket and the lustral water.

Chorus: I agree. I consent. I join in recommending that great

and solemn thanksgivings be addressed to the gods,

and at the same time we sacrifice a little sheep by

way of thanks. Let the Pythian hymn go forth to the

god! Go forth with a song. (The Raven sings).

Pisthetairus: (to the Raven). Stop that cawing! By Heracles! What

commotion. By Zeus, I've heard many horrible

sounds, but not as horrible as this raven. (Enter

Priest). Priest, do your duty! Lead the sacrifice to the

new gods.

Priest: I will do so. Pray to the bird of the hearth, the

guardian of the home, and to the birds and birdesses

of Olympus, each and every cock and hen.

Pisthetairus: O kinglike hawks!

Priest: To the swan of Delphi, and to goldfinch Artemis.

Pisthetairus: Now she's goldfinch-Artemis.

Priest: To other finch gods, and to the ostrich, great mother

of gods and men.

Chorus: To the ostrich, mother of bad actors!

Priest: To give health and security to Cloud-cuckoo-town

                 and all its friendly neighbors.

Pisthetairus: Always include friendly neighbors.

Priest: To the heroic birds and sons of birds; to the pigeon,

                 and the pelican, and the spoonbill, and the pheasant,

                 and the peacock, and the horned owl, and the duck,

                 and the heron, and the stormy petrel, and the black-

                 cap chickadee....

Pisthetairus: Plague take you! Stop calling them! The feast won't

                 be big enough for the flock of vultures you're calling.

                 One bird could eat the whole sacrifice alone. Depart,

                 and I'll finish the offering myself.

Priest: Then I must sing again, devout and holy, and call

                 upon the blessed gods, but only one, for there's only

                 enough to sacrifice to one.

Pisthetairus: Let us pray to the winged gods. (Enter a Poet).

Poet: "Celebrate, o Muse of poetry, in the sweet tones of a

                 hymn, the glory and wealth of Cloud-cuckoo-town."

Pisthetairus: Where did this creature come from? Who are you?

Poet: I am a creator of honey-tongued hymns, a true

                 servant of the Muses, as Homer says.

Pisthetairus: Are you a long-haired poet or a slave?

Poet: I'm a teacher, and a faithful servant of the Muses, as

                 Homer says.

Pisthetairus: You've worn holes in your cloak. Tell me, poet, what

                 misfortune brought you here?

Poet: I have written many beautiful odes to your Cloud-

                 cuckoo-town, with and without rhymes.

Pisthetairus: How long ago did you write them?

Poet: Long, long ago. I've been praising your city for a long

                 time.

Pisthetairus: How can that be? I'm just celebrating its founding

                 now.

Poet: So swift is the information from the Muses, that it travels faster than the swiftest horses. But if you will, noble founder of a great city, nod your head to show that you agree to give me a gift.

Pisthetairus: This pest will cause trouble unless we give him something to get rid of him. (To the Priest). You there, you seem well dressed. Take off some of that clothing and give it to this excellent poet! Take the cloak! Before you freeze to death.

Poet: (putting on cloak). The noble Muse approves your generous gift. But now I want you to consider the verses of Pindar.

Pisthetairus: This fellow won't go.

Poet: "For a poor wanderer, among the nomads, does not have enough clothing." You know what I mean!

Pisthetairus: I understand that you want more. Well, someone

must support the arts. (To the Priest). Strip! (To the

Poet). Take this and depart.

Poet: I'm going. I'll compose some laudatory verses in

honor of your city. "O thou gold-enthroned deity,

rejoice for the chilly and shivering artist. I've left the

frozen wasteland behind, and reached a warmer

clime. Hurray."

Pisthetairus: Yes, by Zeus, but now you've escaped the perils of

frostbite with our help! (Exit Poet). By Zeus, I never

expected news of our city to spread so quickly. (To

the Priest). Prepare the lustral water!

Priest: Let there be a solemn silence! (Enter a Prophet).

Prophet: Do not sacrifice the goat.

Pisthetairus: Who are you?

Prophet: Me? A prophet.

Pisthetairus: May plague take you!

Prophet: Honored sir, do not despise a messenger from the

                  gods, who brings you an ancient oracle that

                  specifically refers to your new city.

Pisthetairus: Then why didn't you tell me these oracles before I

                  founded this city?

Prophet: The gods prevented me.

Pisthetairus: Well, there's no harm in hearing what he has to say.

Prophet: "But when wolves and crows dwell in the same nest,

                  between Corinth and Sicyon...."

Pisthetairus: What do I have to do with Corinth?

Prophet: The gods mean someplace in the air. "First a sacrifice

                  must be offered by a generous man, and whoever

                  comes along first to interpret the meaning, give him

                  a clean cloak, and a new pair of sandals."

Pisthetairus: Do the gods mention the sandals?

Prophet: Soon you shall see. "Give him a fine goblet of wine,

                  and meat from the sacrifice."

Pisthetairus: Do the gods say what kind of meat?

Prophet: Soon you shall see. "And if, o noble and generous

man, you obey this command from the gods, you

shall be an eagle, soaring high above the clouds. But

if you do not give generously, your plans will not take

wing."

Pisthetairus: Do the gods say so?

Prophet: Soon you shall see.

Pisthetairus: Your oracle is different from the one I got from

Apollo. "When a charlatan arrives, uninvited, and

disturbs the people, and demands clothing, food and

gifts, the gods order us to beat him thoroughly."

Prophet: You're babbling nonsense!

Pisthetairus: Soon you shall see! "And don't spare him, even if he

is an eagle from the clouds, but beat him properly."

Prophet: Did the gods really tell you that?

Pisthetairus: Soon you shall see. May plague take you! (beats

him).

Prophet: Alas! Woe is me! (Exits).

Pisthetairus: Take your oracles elsewhere. (Enter Meton, with

mathematical instruments).

Meton: I've come here....

Pisthetairus: Aha! Another pestilence is here! What have you

come here to do? What's the nature of your

business? What's the purpose? What's the meaning

of this visit?

Meton: I wish to survey the air for you, and divide it into

plots.

Pisthetairus: By the gods, who are you?

Meton: Who am I? Meton, famed throughout Greece, and

the rest of the civilized world.

Pisthetairus: Tell me, what are these things?

Meton: Measuring devices for the air. For perceive: the air is

shaped in the form of a funnel, as far as that may be,

thus I, having applied a curved measuring rod from

above, and inserted a compass from below…. Do you

understand?

Pisthetairus: Not at all.

Meton: ….Will measure it with a straight measuring rod,

having applied the principle of squaring the circle,

until the four sides are one, and in the middle is a

market-place, and in order for there to be straight

roads, leading into the precise center, and like the

straight rays of sunlight that emanate from the sun,

which is circular, the beams may shine from it in

every direction.

Pisthetairus: This man is a fraud. Meton!

Meton: What's the matter?

Pisthetairus: Do you know that I admire you? Now take my advice

and sneak away from here quickly!

Meton: What's there to be afraid of?

Pisthetairus: As in Sparta, unwelcome strangers are driven out of

the city, and beaten violently as they leave.

Meton: Is there rioting in the streets?

Pisthetairus: No, by Zeus, certainly not!

Meton: What then?

Pisthetairus: We unanimously determined to punish all imposters.

Meton: I just remembered another appointment.

Pisthetairus: Yes, by Zeus, you'd better, since I don't know if you

can be there soon enough! The beating I warned you

about is coming closer. Here it is! (Beats him).

Meton: How I suffer from fate!

Pisthetairus: Didn't I warn you? Now depart, and survey yourself

somewhere else. (Exit Meton. Enter a Commissioner

with a ballot box).

Commissioner: Where are the officials?

Pisthetairus: Who is this pompous fool?

Commissioner: I've come here as the new commissioner of elections

for Cloud-cuckoo-town, having been appointed by

democratic process.

Pisthetairus: A commissioner? Who sent you here?

Commissioner: The Assembly of Athens sent me on this official

mission.

Pisthetairus: Would you be willing to take your salary, cause no

trouble, and return to where you came from?

Commissioner: Yes, by the gods! I would have preferred to stay at

home and sit in the Assembly, for certain matters of

state require my presence.

Pisthetairus: Take your bribe and depart! Here's your salary!

Commissioner: What's this?

Pisthetairus: Certain matters of state. (Beats him).

Commissioner: I call upon you to bear witness that they have beaten an appointed commissioner.

Pisthetairus: You better depart! And take your ballot boxes with you. (Exit Commissioner). Isn't it shameful? We haven't even sacrificed to the gods yet, and they're already sending their commissioners to our city. (Enter a Seller of decrees, reciting passages from decrees).

Seller: "In the event that a Cloud-cuckoo-townian injure an Athenian."

Pisthetairus: Another pest? Who is this document?

Seller: I'm a seller of decrees, and I've come here to sell you some new laws.

Pisthetairus: What are they?

Seller: "Let the Cloud-cuckoo-townians use the same official measures, weights and decrees as the Olophyxians...."

Pisthetairus: (threatening). You'll soon learn the rules of the

Fistaphyxians.

Seller: What's wrong with you?

Pisthetairus: Won't you take your laws and depart? I'll show you

terrible laws today. (Beats him. Exit Seller. Re- enter

Commissioner).

Commissioner: I summoned Pisthetairus to appear in court next

month, on charges of assault.

Pisthetairus: Not you! What now? Why are you here again?

(Chases him offstage. Exit Commissioner. Re- enter

Seller).

Seller: "But if anyone expels the Archons, and does not

treat them according to the law..."

Pisthetairus: Ah me, long-suffering man! Are you still here?

(Chases him offstage. Exit Seller. Re-enter

Commissioner).

Commissioner: I'll ruin you. I'll sue you for damages, and take everything you own.

Pisthetairus: I'll smash your ballot-boxes.

Commissioner: I'll report you to the Assembly for shitting on the laws of the state. (Exit Commissioner).

Pisthetairus: Bah! Let someone else chase him. (To the Priest). Hello there! Are you ready to continue?

Priest: Let us go into the sacred place and prepare the sacrifice to the gods (Exit Priest and Pisthetairus).

Chorus: Henceforth all mortals shall sacrifice to me, the all-seeing ruler of everything, with votive prayers. I guard the entire earth, and protect the thriving fruits, slaying the insects that lurk in the earth and trees, and devour the fruit with the all- consuming jaws, as it grows from the bud. I destroy those insects that blight sweet-smelling gardens, and all reptiles and poisonous beasts will be slaughtered by my winged power of beak and talon. This day shall be famous for special proclamations: "If anyone resists a tyrant he will be richly rewarded." The next proclamation: "If anyone kills a bird hunter he will be richly rewarded.", but if you capture him alive, you get twice the reward, because he ties the birds together and sells them; because he inflates the thrushes to make them fat, and plucks them bald, and shoves their feathers in the blackbird beaks; because he also traps pigeons, and keeps them locked in a coop, and uses them as decoys to trap other pigeons. We therefore make this proclamation: "That if anyone is keeping birds imprisoned at home, we order you to set them free. If you do not obey, we birds will arrest you, put you in chains, and use you as decoys to trap other men." Blessed is the race of winged birds, who wear no cloaks in winter, nor do the hot rays of the sun scorch our feathers, for we

dwell in the leaves of the flowery meadows, while

the divine grasshopper, maddened by the noontime

sun, sings its impassioned song. We spend the winter

in hollow caves, cavorting with the mountain

nymphs. In spring we feed upon pure myrtle-berries,

and the garden herbs of the Graces. We wish to issue

a final proclamation to the critics, about how we'll

reward them. If they praise us, they'll receive better

gifts than the renowned Paris. First, what every critic

needs, a plump owl that hatches money instead of

eggs. Next, they'll live in the rafters of theatres, then

if they wish to steal anything from a playwright, we'll

give them a clever hawk with fast claws. Last, we'll

send them special delicacies to eat. But if they don't

praise us, and tell our audiences wonderful things

about us, they'd better cover themselves wherever

they go, for the birds will get revenge by shitting on their heads. (Re-enter Pisthetairus).

Pisthetairus: O birds, the omens are favorable, but why hasn't a messenger come from the wall to tell us what's going on there? But look! Someone's running like an Olympic sprinter! (Enter First Messenger).

1st Messenger: Where, where, where is…. Where is he? Where is he? Where is Pisthetairus, our leader?

Pisthetairus: Here I am!

1st Messenger: The wall is done.

Pisthetairus: You bring good news.

1st Messenger: It is the most beautiful and most magnificent wall ever built. It's so wide, that two charioteers could drive past each other in opposite directions, using horses as large as the wooden horse of Troy.

Pisthetairus: O Heracles!

1st Messenger: And it's so long, for I measured it, that it's longer
than the longest wall ever built.

Pisthetairus: O Poseidon! What a length! Who built something
that huge?

1st Messenger: Birds. No one else. No Egyptian bricklayers, stone-
masons, carpenters. Just birds. Thirty thousand
cranes flew from Libya with stones in their beaks for
the foundation. Spoonbills chiseled the stones in
place. Ten thousand storks made bricks, and other
water birds brought them to the wall.

Pisthetairus: But who carried mortar for them?

1st Messenger: Herons, in hods.

Pisthetairus: How did they get the mortar in the hods?

1st Messenger: This, noble sir, was done cleverly. The geese used
their feet like shovels, and threw the mortar in the
hods.

Pisthetairus: Then what couldn't feet do next?

1st Messenger: Then, by Zeus, ducks wearing aprons, carried bricks,

and apprentice swallows carrying trowels flew with

mortar in their mouths.

Pisthetairus: Why should anyone ever hire laborers again? What

happened next? Who finished the woodwork?

1st Messenger: The Pelicans were clever carpenters, who chopped

out the gates with their bills, and the chopping

sounded like a shipyard. Then gates were put in, with

locks, and guards were posted on the watchtowers,

and inspected regularly. But now that you have my

news, I'll go and wash, and leave the rest to you. (Exit

1st Messenger).

Chorus: (to Pisthetairus). Ho, you! What are you doing? Are

you surprised that the wall was built so quickly?

Pisthetairus: Yes, by the gods, I am. For it's so wonderful that it

hardly seems possible. But look! Here comes a guard

as if chased by enemies! (Enter 2nd Messenger).

2nd Messenger: Oh, oh! Oh, oh!

Pisthetairus: What's wrong?

2nd Messenger: Something terrible has happened! For just now one

of the gods sent by Zeus, flew through our airspace

into the city, and wasn't noticed by the Bluejays, who

were on guard.

Pisthetairus: O what a dreadful, wicked deed! Which god is it?

2nd Messenger: We don't know. But we know he has wings.

Pisthetairus: Did you send a patrol to find him?

2nd Messenger: Yes! We sent thirty thousand hawks, falcons, eagles,

vultures and turkeys. The air is filled with whirring

wings seeking the god, who can't be very far from

here. (Exit 2nd Messenger).

Pisthetairus: We must arm ourselves! Advance! Retreat! Attack!

Bring me a weapon!

Chorus: It's war! Total war between birds and gods. On

guard, all of you. Protect our precious clouded air, so

none of the gods can get by unnoticed. Look around,

all of you. Be alert! For I can hear the sound of the

flapping wings of the god.

Pisthetairus: (Enter Iris). Ho, you! Where are you flying? Stop

flying! Be quiet! Stand still! Stop flapping your wings!

Who are you? From what country? You better tell me

where you're from.

Iris: I come from the gods, on Olympus.

Pisthetairus: What's your name?

Iris: Iris the swift. But what do you want?

Pisthetairus: Let the falcon guards seize her.

Iris: Seize me? Who in the world is this dolt?

Pisthetairus: You'll pay for that.

Iris: This is absurd.

Pisthetairus: O most abominable criminal! Through what gates did

you enter our city?

Iris: By Zeus, I don't know what you mean.

Pisthetairus: Did you hear how she pretends to be innocent? Did

you ask the jackdaw-guards for permission to enter?

Won't you speak? Do you have a passport from the

storks?

Iris: What?

Pisthetairus: Did you get a passport?

Iris: Are you demented?

Pisthetairus: Did a bird customs officer stamp you with his seal?

Iris: By Zeus, no one stamped me anywhere, you insolent

wretch!

Pisthetairus: Then pray tell me, in these circumstances, why are

you flying through a foreign city and its atmosphere,

in silence?

Iris: How else should the gods fly?

Pisthetairus: I don't know, by Zeus, but certainly not like that. And

even now you're not being punished. Do you know

that if you were punished according to your crime,

you would have been arrested, condemned and put
to death as a lesson to all Irises?

Iris: But I'm an immortal god!

Pisthetairus: Nevertheless, you would have been publicly
executed. For truthfully, we'd be in trouble with
everyone we ruled, if you gods led a life of pleasure
and licentiousness, and refused to obey your
superiors. But where were you flying?

Iris: Me? I'm flying to mankind, from Zeus my father, to
arrange sacrifices to the Olympic gods, to offer sheep
upon the sacred altars, and to fill the air with the
vapors of burnt sacrifices.

Pisthetairus: What did you say? To what gods?

Iris: What gods? To us, the gods in heaven.

Pisthetairus: Are you gods?

Iris: Who else are gods?

Pisthetairus: The birds are gods now, and men must sacrifice to them, but by Zeus, not to Zeus!

Iris: O fool! Fool! Don't stir the dreadful wrath of the gods, or justice, at the hands of Zeus, may bring destruction to your entire race, and consume your bodies and reduce your houses to ashes with fiery thunderbolts.

Pisthetairus: How dare you! Stop babbling! Be quiet! What an outrage! Do you think you're scaring a dumb foreigner with those threats? If Zeus annoys me anymore, I'll send fire-bearing eagles to his palace, and reduce it to ashes. I'll send six hundred great heroes, clad in leopard-skins, to demolish Olympus. That would cause him trouble! And if you annoy me any further, I'll spread your legs, and ravish you myself. You'd be astonished that an old man could be so vigorous.

Iris: Curse you, you wretch, and your filthy words!

Pisthetairus: Be off with you. Go quickly. Shoo! Shoo!

Iris: By my virtue, my father will make you pay for your

                 insolence!

Pisthetairus: Ah, miserable me! Fly off, and find a younger man to

                 satisfy your fires. (Exit Iris).

Chorus: We have rejected Zeus and the other gods, and they

                 can no longer pass through our city. And men

                 throughout the earth, can no longer send up the

                 smoke of sacrifices to the gods, through our city.

Pisthetairus: I'm afraid that the herald sent to men will not return.

                 (Enter Herald).

Herald: Hail Pisthetairus! Blessed of men! The wisest! The

                 most illustrious! The most subtle! The wisest! The

                 most illustrious! I'm at your orders!

Pisthetairus: What is the news?

Herald: All mankind honors and reveres you, and sends you

                   this golden crown for your wisdom.

Pisthetairus: I accept it. But why do they honor me?

Herald: O you who founded our illustrious city in the sky! You

                   don't know how many men honor you, and how

                   many admire this new city. Before you founded this

                   city everyone imitated the Spartans: long hair, dirty

                   bodies, carried canes, ate special herbs, and

                   pretended to live like Socrates. But now everyone is

                   bird mad, and they take pleasure in pretending to be

                   birds. Everyone gets out of bed in the morning and

                   "flies off" about their business. They eat together in

                   flocks, and they all live in nests. The fad has spread

                   so fast that everyone is giving themselves bird

                   names. If you don't sleep at night, you're a night owl.

                   If you're silly, you're a goose. There are blind bats

                   and old crows. The mad passion for birds has

everyone singing and chirping. Thus is the state of affairs on earth. But I must warn you: thousands of men are planning to come here for wings. So you'd better get a big supply of feathers for the newcomers.

Pisthetairus: By Zeus, there's no more time to stand around and talk. But go as quickly as you can, and gather wings. I will receive our visitors. (Exit Herald).

Chorus: Soon our city's population will grow.

Pisthetairus: Let good fortune follow us!

Chorus: I am filled with love for our city.

Pisthetairus: (to Manes). I order you to bring wings quickly.

Chorus: What advantage can't you find in this city, that would make a man want to live here. Wisdom, love, Ambrosial Graces and the cheerful face of gentle-minded tranquility.

Pisthetairus: (to Manes). How lazily you serve me! Won't you
move faster?

Chorus: Let someone quickly bring a basket of wings. And
wake him up by beating him soundly! For he's
exceptionally sluggish, like a dumb donkey.

Pisthetairus: Yes, Manes is lazy.

Chorus: First arrange the wings in their proper order; musical
ones for songbirds, prophetic ones, nautical ones for
seabirds, and be certain that you give men wings
according to their nature.

Pisthetairus: (to Manes). By the Kestrels, I certainly won't refrain
from beating you since you're so lazy and shiftless.
(Enter Parracide).

Parracide: Would I might be a high-soaring eagle, so I might fly
over the billowing waves of the desolate blue sea.

Pisthetairus: The messenger seems to have told the truth, for here
comes someone singing about eagles!

Parracide: Heigh ho! There is nothing sweeter than flying.

                 Truthfully, I adore the laws of the birds, for I'm bird-

                 mad, and flight mad, and want to live with you and

                 obey your laws.

Pisthetairus: What laws? For the birds have many laws.

Parracide: All of them. But there's a special one about pecking

                 and strangling one's father.

Pisthetairus: Yes, by Zeus, we consider it very manly here, if a

                 chick beats its father.

Parracide: I really migrated here because of this, for I want to

                 strangle my father and possess all his goods.

Pisthetairus: But we birds have an ancient law inscribed in the

                 tablets of the storks. "When the father stork has

                 raised his brood and taught all the young storks to

                 fly, the young birds in turn, must support their

                 father."

Parracide: By Zeus, I won't do very well here, if I still must

support my father.

Pisthetairus: Not at all. Since you came here in good faith, dear sir,

I will present you with wings as a public reward. I

won't give you bad advice, young man. I'll teach you

what I learned when I was a child: "Don't beat your

father, but take these wings and imagine you are a

bird; guard your city, serve in the army, support

yourself on your pay, and let your father live." Since

you are aggressive and like to fight, fly away to the

towns on the borders of Thrace, and fight there.

Parracide: By Dionysus, you know what you're talking about,

and I'll obey you.

Pisthetairus: By Zeus, this shows you have some sense. (Exit

Parracide. Enter Cinesias, singing one of his own

compositions).

Cinesias: "I soar aloft on gossamer wings, to Olympus, and

                 flutter from one melodious strain to another...."

Pisthetairus: This fellow needs a boat-load of wings to stay afloat.

Cinesias: ".... pursuing a new tune, fearless in mind and body."

Pisthetairus: We welcome Cinesias, who's thin as a rail. Why do

                 you move around in circles?

Cinesias: "I wish to become a bird, the pure-voiced

                 nightingale."

Pisthetairus: Stop singing, and tell me what you mean.

Cinesias: I want you to equip me with wings, so I can fly aloft

                 in the sky, and get some new air- buffed, snow-

                 shined songs from the clouds.

Pisthetairus: Why should you want songs from the clouds?

Cinesias: Indeed, my profession depends on them, for the

                 splendid dithrambic songs are misty, duskyish, dark

                 gleaming, high-flown and cloudy. But you'll

understand soon enough when you hear them.

(Prepares to sing).

Pisthetairus: Oh, no. Absolutely not!

Cinesias: Yes, by Heracles, you shall; for I will fly across the

entire sky and sing. "Ye winged forms of ether-

skimming, long-necked birds...."

Pisthetairus: Ahoy there!

Cinesias: "... .who leap across the surging sea, may I go with

the gusting wind...."

Pisthetairus: By Zeus, I swear I'll stop your gusts.

Cinesias: ".... one time ascending towards the southern path,

another time transporting my body to the god of the

winds, plowing furrows in the harborless heavens."

(Cinesias turns to Pisthetairus, who comes behind

him and flaps him on the head with his wings). You

think that's a clever way to stop me?

Pisthetairus: Why? Aren't you pleased at being fanned by wings?

Cinesias: Is this how you treat the teacher of the official state

Chorus, whose services are always in demand?

Pisthetairus: Then are you willing to stay with us, and train the

eggs of flying birds to be a chorus?

Cinesias: It's obvious that you are mocking me. Yet to be

assured, I won't stop singing until I'm equipped with

wings to soar through the sky. (Exit Cinesias. Enter

Informer, singing).

Informer: "O long-winged, dappled swallow, o motley-

feathered bird, possessing nothing!"

Pisthetairus: We've spread a terrible disease. Here comes another

warbler!

Informer: I repeat the refrain: "O long-winged, dappled

swallow!"

Pisthetairus: He appears to be singing about new clothes, and a

lot of swallows.

Informer: Who is the man that provides wings to newcomers?

Pisthetairus: Here I am! Tell me what you want.

Informer: I want wings, wings. Don't ask me again.

Pisthetairus: Do you intend to fly off for a new cloak?

Informer: No, by Zeus, I'm an informer, and I travel the islands

                 delivering summons....

Pisthetairus: A fortunate man in such a profession!

Informer: .... And I'm a blackmailer. Therefore, I want wings so I

                 can deliver summons faster to more cities.

Pisthetairus: How'll you deliver summons better with wings?

Informer: Not better, by Zeus, but I'll avoid pirates by returning

                 from errands with the cranes, after swallowing many

                 law-suits for ballast.

Pisthetairus: Why do you do such work? Tell me why a young man

                 is an informer.

Informer: What else can I do? I don't want to dig ditches.

Pisthetairus: By Zeus, there are many other honest occupations

                 for a young man without stirring up law-suits.

Informer: My good sir, don't criticize me. Give me wings.

Pisthetairus: Indeed, my words are giving you wings.

Informer: But how could words give a man wings?

Pisthetairus: Words make everyone sprout wings.

Informer: Everyone?

Pisthetairus: Haven't you heard fathers talking in the barber

                shops, telling about how their sons sprout wings?

                Another one says his son has winged-off to be an

                actor, and his mind has already become flighty.

Informer: They sprout wings from words?

Pisthetairus: Certainly. For with words, the mind is excited and the

                man is elated. Thus I also want to set you on wings

                with good words, and aim you towards a legitimate

                occupation.

Informer: But I'm not willing.

Pisthetairus: Then what will you do?

Informer: I won't disgrace my heritage. My grandfather was a

                 professional informer. Come, equip me with light,

                 swift wings, like a hawk, so after I deliver a summons

                 to a foreigner, then bring a charge against him at

                 court, I can fly away before he appears.

Pisthetairus: I understand what you mean; so the foreigner will be

                 condemned before he arrives.

Informer: (delighted and rubbing his hands). You understand

                 perfectly.

Pisthetairus: Then he sails here, while you fly back to his city and

                 seize his goods.

Informer: You understand everything. You have to keep

                 spinning like a top.

Pisthetairus: I understand a top. Well, by Zeus, I have a special set

                 of wings. (Produces the horsewhip).

Informer: Ah what misery! You've got a whip.

Pisthetairus: No, it's a pair of wings, and I'll make you spin like a

top today. (Beats him).

Informer: Oh what misery!

Pisthetairus: Won't you fly away from here? Won't you vanish and

let a demon take you? Soon you'll have a bitter taste

of your own harsh justice, you rascal. (Beats him off

the stage. Exit Informer). Let's collect the wings and

depart.

Chorus: Many strange and wondrous things have we seen

and flown over! For there's a tree without courage

that grows far away, like a large, cowardly, useless

citizen, who blooms in spring by informing on his

neighbors; but in winter sheds his shield, that should

protect his city. Then there is a place of eternal

darkness, far from the solitary flicker of lamplight,

where men consort and dine with heroes, except at

evening. Then it's no longer safe to meet them; for if

a mortal man were to meet Orestes the hero at night, he would be stripped and beaten on his noble parts. (Enter Prometheus, cloaked and under an umbrella).

Prometheus: Woe is me! I'm afraid that Zeus will see me. Where is Pisthetairus?

Pisthetairus: Ha! Who's this? What's the disguise for?

Prometheus: Do you see any of the gods following me?

Pisthetairus: No, by Zeus, I don't. But who are you?

Prometheus: What time is it?

Pisthetairus: What time? A little after twelve. But who are you?

Prometheus: Afternoon or night?

Pisthetairus: You're annoying me!

Prometheus: What is Zeus doing? Is he gathering or scattering rainclouds?

Pisthetairus: Plague take you! (Threatens Prometheus).

Prometheus: Under these circumstances, I'll reveal myself.

(Uncovers).

Pisthetairus: O dear Prometheus!

Prometheus: Stop! Stop! Don't shout!

Pisthetairus: What's the matter?

Prometheus: Be quiet! Don't say my name! For if Zeus saw me

here he'd destroy me. Hold the umbrella over my

head, so the gods don't see me while I tell you what's

going on in heaven.

Pisthetairus: Ha! Ha! You've used forethought for a clever plan.

(Holds the umbrella). Come under quickly! Now

speak up confidently!

Prometheus: Then listen!

Pisthetairus: I'm listening. Speak!

Prometheus: Zeus is ruined

Pisthetairus: When was he ruined?

Prometheus: When you colonized the sky. For no one sacrifices to the gods any more; nor has the savory odor of burnt thighs reached us since that time. We fast without sacrifices, as if it's the ceremony of Thesmophoria. Meanwhile, all the barbarian gods are ravenous with hunger, and they're shrieking that they'll make war on Zeus if he doesn't arrange to have the portals of heaven re-opened to let the sacrifices pass through.

Pisthetairus: Are there any other barbarian gods besides you?

Prometheus: Yes, so citizens without the proper ancestry can worship barbarian gods.

Pisthetairus: What are they called?

Prometheus: They're called Triballi.

Pisthetairus: I understand, that's where tribulations come from.

Prometheus: Certainly. But I'll tell you something plainly. Ambassadors are coming from Zeus and the Triballi to arrange a truce. But don't make peace unless Zeus

agrees to restore power to the birds, and give you
Basileia for your wife.

Pisthetairus: Who's Basileia?

Prometheus: A most beautiful maiden, who tends Zeus' thunderbolts, and other affairs of state; good counsel, good
government, moderation, the ship-yards, freedom of
speech, payroll clerks and the price of theatre
tickets.

Pisthetairus: Then she manages everything for him.

Prometheus: She does. If you get her away from him, you'll control
everything. This is what I've come to tell you about,
for I've always been generously disposed towards
mankind.

Pisthetairus: Yes, because you alone of all the gods gave us fire.

Prometheus: As you know, I hate all the Olympian gods.

Pisthetairus: Yes, by Zeus, but the gods always detested you.

Prometheus: But in order for me to return to heaven undetected,

bring my umbrella, so even if Zeus should see me,

he'd think I was attending a religious festival.

Pisthetairus: Take this and go. (Exit Prometheus).

Chorus: Near a far away kingdom there is a lake, where the

unwashed Socrates invokes the dead. Cowardly

citizens, who did not do their duty to the state while

they were alive, go there. They sacrifice to the spirits

of the dead, like Odysseus. And then, from the

underworld, there ascended a flock of bats. (Enter

Poseidon, Heracles, Triballus).

Poseidon: Look! Right in front of our eyes, it's Cloud-cuckoo-

town, where we're going as ambassadors. (To

Triballus). Ho there, you! What are you doing? Must

you wear your cloak like that? Make yourself look

presentable. (Triballus makes himself look worse).

What an ill-bred lout! You definitely represent the

common man. O democracy! Where will you lead us,

if this creature was elected an ambassador from the

gods.

Triballus: (grunts and mumbles).

Poseidon: Plague take you! For I see you are by far the most

barbarous of all the gods. Tell me now, Heracles,

what should we do?

Heracles: I told you already that I'd like to strangle the fellow,

whoever he is, who built the walls that keep out the

gods.

Poseidon: But my good sir, we've come here as ambassadors,

to arrange a truce.

Heracles: I'd like to strangle him twice as much!

Pisthetairus: (pretending not to see them). Bring the cheese-

grater, the cheese, savoury spices and stir up the

cooking fires.

Heracles: We three gods greet you.

Pisthetairus: (without looking at them). Hurry! Cover them with

that special, delicious sauce.

Heracles: What are you cooking?

Pisthetairus: Certain plump birds who have been found guilty of

rebelling against the democratic party.

Heracles: Why do you cover them with sauce first?

Pisthetairus: (pretending to see him for the first time). O

welcome, Heracles! What are you doing here?

Heracles: We've come as ambassadors from the gods to end

this war. (Enter Servant).

Servant: There's just enough cooking oil left.

Pisthetairus: Good. The birds won't roast tenderly without being

basted with oil.

Heracles: We gods don't gain anything by making war, and if

you were friendly with us gods, we'd always give you

pure drinking water and balmy weather in winter.

We've come with complete authority to negotiate all the issues.

Pisthetairus: But don't forget that we didn't start the war. Yet now, if you are agreeable, we're willing to make peace, if you're willing to do what's fair and proper. These are our terms: "That Zeus restore rulership to us birds." If you agree to these terms, I'll invite the ambassadors to a special feast.

Heracles: I agree! And cast my vote....

Poseidon: What, you scoundrel! You're a fool and a glutton. Would you give away your father's kingdom for a meal?

Pisthetairus: That's not so! Won't you gods be more powerful if the birds rule the earth? Presently, mortals hide under the clouds, and swear falsely by the gods. But if the birds are your allies, whenever anyone swears falsely by the raven and Zeus, the raven will sneak up on the perjurer, then fly at him and peck out his

eyes.

Poseidon: By Poseidon, well said!

Heracles: I think so too.

Pisthetairus: (to Triballus). What do you say?

Triballus: (grunts and mumbles).

Heracles: He says he agrees.

Poseidon: If both of you approve this treaty, I agree too.

Heracles: Ho you! We agree to restore power to the birds.

Pisthetairus: By Zeus, there's something that I almost forgot. I'll

allow Zeus to keep Hera, but I must receive the

maiden Basileia for my wife.

Poseidon: You don't really want peace. Let us depart for home.

(Turns to leave).

Pisthetairus: I don't care. (Shouting). Cook, be sure the sauce is

sweet.

Heracles: (stops Poseidon by the arm). My dearest friend, Poseidon! Where are you rushing off to? Shall we have another Trojan War for one woman?

Poseidon: What should we do?

Heracles: We should make peace.

Poseidon: You pathetic creature! Don't you realize that you've been deceived during all our negotiations? Truthfully, you're hurting yourself; for you should inherit all of Zeus' possessions at his death. But if Zeus dies after you've given power to the birds, you'll be a beggar.

Pisthetairus: (taking Heracles aside). Alas, what misery! How he's cheating you! Come a little closer so I can tell you something privately! My poor fellow, your uncle Poseidon is deceiving you; for according to the law, you've no right to your father's property, not a claim; for you're a bastard, born out of wedlock.

Heracles: I'm a bastard! What do you mean?

Pisthetairus: Yes you, by Zeus, since you're the son of a foreign

woman, otherwise, how could Athene be a legal

heiress, since she's a daughter, if there were

brothers born in wedlock?

Heracles: But what if my father gives me the natural son's

inheritance at his death?

Pisthetairus: The law forbids him to do that. This Poseidon here,

who's getting you excited, will be the first one to

claim your father's property, saying that he is a

brother born in wedlock. And now I'll also recite the

law of Solon for you: "A bastard may not inherit his

father's estate, if there are children born in wedlock,

then the nearest kin by birth shall claim the

property."

Heracles: Then I have no claim to my father's property?

Pisthetairus: Certainly not, by Zeus! But tell me, did your father

                 ever introduce you to the other gods as his heir?

Heracles: He never did! And I've been wondering about that

                 for a long time.

Pisthetairus: Why bother looking up and glaring daggers? But join

                 us and I'll appoint you an official, and supply you

                 with bird's milk and other delicacies.

Heracles: Once again you've spoken justly about the maiden,

                 and I vote to deliver her to you.

Pisthetairus: (to Poseidon). What did you say?

Poseidon: I vote against it.

Pisthetairus: Everything's up to Triballus. (to Triballus). How do

                 you vote?

Triballus: (Grunts and mumbles).

Heracles: He says he votes to give her up.

Poseidon: No, by Zeus, he didn't vote yes, unless he voted to

                 make her a swallow.

Pisthetairus: Therefore he says he voted to make her a swallow.

Poseidon: Now both of you arrange peace and come to an agreement. And since both of you are deciding everything, I won't say anything else.

Heracles: (to Pisthetairus). We've decided to concede all the issues you mentioned. But you come with us to heaven, so you can claim Basileia, and everything else there.

Pisthetairus: Then the rebellious birds were killed in time to be roasted for my wedding feast.

Heracles: (to Poseidon). Would you mind if I remained here and roasted the birds, while you went ahead.

Poseidon: You're roasting the birds? You're showing terrible gluttony. Won't you go back with us?

Heracles: I'd be well fed, indeed! Where's the kitchen? (Exit Heracles).

Pisthetairus: Come then, let some one get me a marriage-cloak.

(Exit Pisthetairus, Poseidon and Triballus).

Chorus: Beyond the rugged mountains there is a knavish race

who live by the cleverness of their speech. They

reap, sow and gather the harvest earned by their

speech; suspicion and distrust. They are treacherous

and greedy, and confuse honest citizens with their

speech. That's why when sacrifices are offered to the

gods, the tongue is cut out from the root. (Enter a

Messenger).

Messenger: O you who flourish in all ways, far more than words

describe, o thrice happy winged race of birds, receive

your sovereign in regal splendor. For he's

approaching, shining forth like a bright-burning star

in the gold-gleaming dome of heaven. Nor have the

shimmering brilliance of sunbeams ever blazed forth,

as in the radiant beauty of the woman accompanying

him, brandishing the winged thunderbolt of Zeus. And an indescribable perfume permeates heaven's vault…. A wondrous spectacle! And puffs of incense blow away the plume of smoke. But look! Here is the master! Come, let us sing an appropriate, sacred song of the goddess muse. (Enter Pisthetairus and Basileia, gorgeously appareled).

Chorus: Move back, part ranks, step aside, get out of the way, fly around the happy man of good fortune! Oh, oh. What loveliness! What beauty! O you, who have arranged a most blessed marriage that will benefit our city! Great, great blessings have come to the race of birds from this man. Come, receive him and his Basileia with wedding songs and bridal odes. Once upon a time the Fates and the gods betrothed Zeus, the great ruler of the lofty thrones, to Olympian Hera, with a wedding song. O hymen. O Hymenaus!

And shining Eros, god of love, with golden wings,

guided the nuptial chariot of Zeus and happy Hera.

"O Hymen. O Hymenaeus."

Pisthetairus: I'm delighted with your hymns and songs, and I

admire your words! Come now, celebrate this

occasion of my getting the dreadful, bright

thunderbolt of Zeus himself.

Chorus: O mighty blaze of lightning! O immortal, fiery

weapon of Zeus! O thunders that echo across the

earth, bringing rain and shaking the sky! From you

this man possesses all, even Basileia, the helper of

Zeus. "O Hymen. O Hymenaeus!"

Pisthetairus: Join the wedding procession, all my winged

followers! Come to the kingdom of heaven for the

wedding feast. Now take my hand, o blessed bride,

and let your wings join mine in sacred dance, and I

will exalt you.

Chorus: Alala! Io Paean! Hurrah! Victory to the highest of the

gods! (Exit all).

Lysistrata

Lysistrata:	Well! If I asked them to meet me at the temple of Dionysus for an orgy, I wouldn't be able to get in the door because of the crowd. Yet there's not a woman in sight. But here comes my neighbor. (Enter Calonice). Good morning, Calonice!
Calonice:	Good morning, Lysistrata. What's bothering you? Don't look so angry, child. Frowning makes you unattractive.
Lysistrata:	I'm furious, Calonice, and distressed that the women are behaving just as badly as men describe us....
Calonice:	That's what we're like!
Lysistrata:	I arranged a meeting to discuss urgent business, yet they're still lingering in bed.

Calonice: They'll come, my dear. It's so difficult for women to
              get away from the house. There are husbands to be
              tended, servants to be watched, children to be
              washed, fed and soothed.

Lysistrata: But there are more important things for them to do.

Calonice: Tell me why you've summoned the women, dear
              Lysistrata. What's the problem? How big is it?

Lysistrata: Enormous.

Calonice: Is it thick?

Lysistrata: Very!

Calonice: Then why didn't we come?

Lysistrata: That's not what I meant. If it were that big there
              would have been a stampede to get here first. It's
              something that I've been tossing and turning over for
              many sleepless nights.

Calonice: You must be worn out and fragile.

Lysistrata: Yes. So fragile that the safety of Greece depends on

us women.

Calonice: On women? What a fragile hope!

Lysistrata: The destiny of the state is in our hands! We could

destroy the Spartans....

Calonice: Then let them perish.

Lysistrata: And the Boeotians....

Calonice: Not completely. Spare their delicious eels.

Lysistrata: For Athens' sake I'd never do anything that terrible,

believe me. But if the Spartans and Boeotian women

join us, together we'll save Greece.

Calonice: What brilliant or daring deed could we women do?

We're more accustomed to leading sheltered lives,

wearing beautiful clothes, delicate sandals and

transparent tops.

Lysistrata: These are the weapons that will serve us: clothes,

perfumes, sandals, cosmetics, especially see-through

garments.

Calonice: How?

Lysistrata: So that no man raises a spear against another....

Calonice: By the goddesses, I'll get a new dress!

Lysistrata: Or takes a shield....

Calonice: I'll wear a see-through vest!

Lysistrata: Or lifts a sword....

Calonice: I'll buy new sandals!

Lysistrata: But why aren't the women here yet?

Calonice: They should have been here long ago.

Lysistrata: My dear, you see they're true Athenians; always late.

But I don't see any of the women no matter where I

look.

Calonice: They're probably still underneath their husbands.

Lysistrata: Not even our nearest neighbors who should be here

first.

Calonice: But here comes Theogenes' wife, and others. Who

are they?

Lysistrata: They come from Anagyra.

Calonice: They usually come first. (Enter Myrrhine and others).

Myrrhine: Are we late, Lysistrata? Don't you have anything to

say? Why so silent?

Lysistrata: I can't welcome you cheerfully, Myrrhine, when

you're this late for an important meeting.

Myrrhine: I couldn't find my clothes in the dark. But if this

business is so important, tell us about it.

Lysistrata: Let's wait for the women from Boeotia and Sparta.

Myrrhine: You're right. Look! Here comes Lampito. (Enter

Lampito).

Lysistrata: Welcome Lampito! Oh dearest Spartan. How you glow with healthy beauty! What clear skin! You could easily strangle a bull.

Lampito: By the goddesses, I could! I exercise daily and stretch my buttocks.

Lysistrata: What beautiful breasts you have!

Lampito: You're handling me like a sacrificial offering. (Enter Boeotian).

Lysistrata: What country is this woman from?

Lampito: Boeotia.

Lysistrata: By Zeus, what glorious hair!

Calonice: She keeps hers neatly plucked. (Enter Corinthian).

Lysistrata: Who's this?

Lampito: A Corinthian. But an innocent one.

Lysistrata: She certainly has some innocent looking parts!

Lampito: But who summoned us here?

Lysistrata: I did!

Lampito: Then tell us what you want.

Myrrhine: What's so important about this meeting?

Lysistrata: I'll tell you. But first I have a question.

Myrrhine: Anything.

Lysistrata: Do you yearn for your husbands who are absent on

              military service? For I know that they're all far away.

Calonice: My poor husband has been gone for five months.

Lysistrata: Mine has been gone for seven months.

Lampito: Even when my husband comes back from the war, no

              sooner is he home, then he picks up his shield and is

              off again.

Lysistrata: The only men left are too old for us. I haven't seen

              anything big enough to console us in the absence of

              our husbands. Now, if I find a way to end the war,

              would you help me?

Myrrhine: By the goddesses, I will! Even if I have to pawn my

              clothes and drink the money today.

Calonice: I'll fillet myself like a fish, and give half away.

Lampito: I'll climb the highest mountain for a glimpse of

               peace.

Lysistrata: Then I'll tell you what we must do to force the men

               to make peace. We must abstain....

Myrrhine: From what? Tell us!

Lysistrata: Will you do it?

Myrrhine: We'll do it, even if we die from it!

Lysistrata: Then we must abstain from all sex with our men.

               Why are you turning away from me? Where are you

               going? Why are you clenching your teeth and shaking

               your heads? Why are you frowning and starting to

               cry? Will you do it, or not?

Myrrhine: I can't do it. Let the war go on!

Calonice: Neither can I! Let the war go on!

Lysistrata: How could you say this, you poor fish? You just

               offered to cut yourself in half.

Calonice: Ask anything else, anything. Whatever you want. I'll

walk through fire if I must, rather than give up sex;

for there's nothing else like it, dearest Lysistrata.

Lysistrata: (To Myrrhine). What do you say?

Myrrhine: I'll also walk through fire.

Lysistrata: Women are so immoral! No wonder poets write

tragedies about us, for we're not fit to be anything

but love objects! But my dear Spartan, join me! For if

you alone help me, we might end the war.

Lampito: By the goddesses. It's hard for women to sleep alone

without their men. But we need peace.

Lysistrata: O dearest of women, you're the only brave one here!

Calonice: But if we abstain from sex, may heaven forbid, would

that bring peace?

Lysistrata: Certainly! For if we paint our faces suggestively,

pluck the hair from our bodies and wear transparent

vests that show our nipples, the men would go wild

with lust, get erections and try to mount us immediately. Then we'll simply refuse. They'll make peace instantly!

Lampito: It's true! When fierce Menelaus saw Helen's naked breasts, he meekly put down his sword.

Myrrhine: But dear friend, what if our husbands leave us?

Lysistrata: They won't stray very far.

Calonice: This is idle chit-chat. What if they drag us to bed and try to rape us?

Lysistrata: Hold onto the door.

Calonice: What if they beat us?

Lysistrata: Submit passively. They won't get any pleasure if you make them force you. Besides, you want to frustrate them. They won't remain stiff and eager if you're indifferent, and they won't enjoy them-selves if you don't respond.

Calonice: If both of you are determined to do this, the rest of
us agree.

Lampito: We'll persuade our husbands to make and keep an
honest peace. But how could anyone convince these
warlike Athenians to reach an agreement?

Lysistrata: We'll see that our city makes peace.

Lampito: Not as long as their warships are armed and ready,
and their treasury has enough money to finance the
war.

Lysistrata: I've considered the problem carefully. At this very
moment while we're discussing the plan, the old
women of Athens are pretending to offer a public
sacrifice, and they'll seize the Acropolis, with all the
money in the treasury.

Lampito: The way you describe it, the plan might really
succeed.

Lysistrata: Then, Lampito, we should swear an inviolable oath that binds us together.

Lampito: Tell us the oath so we may swear.

Lysistrata: Well said. Where is our shield bearer? What are you gaping at? We have to place a shield upside down, and add the sacrificial parts.

Calonice: Lysistrata, what kind of oath are we swearing?

Lysistrata: What? We'll sacrifice a sheep over a shield, the way they do in tragedies.

Calonice: We shouldn't swear to make peace over a shield.

Lysistrata: Then what oath should we take?

Calonice: We could sacrifice a white stallion.

Lysistrata: Where can we get a white stallion?

Calonice: What else could we do?

Lysistrata: By Zeus, I'll tell you. Let's place a large bowl on the ground, and cut the throat.... Of a jar of wine, and swear not to dilute the wine with water.

Lampito: O Mother Earth! I praise your oath.

Lysistrata: (To one of the women). Fetch a bowl and a jar of

              wine.

Calonice: O dear women, what a huge jar! Anyone would get

              excited seeing this.

Lysistrata: Put down the bowl, and everyone take hold of the

              victim. Goddess of Persuasion, and bowl that hallows

              friendship, receive our offering, and grant the

              women's wish. (Calonice pours the wine into the

              bowl).

Calonice: The blood is an excellent color and flows well.

Lampito: (bends and sniffs the bowl). It smells delicious.

Lysistrata: Allow me to swear first. (Tries to drink from the

              bowl).

Calonice: No, by Aphrodite. Not unless we choose and you win.

Lysistrata: Lampito, lift the bowl. All of you hold it. Calonice,

              you speak for everyone, and repeat what I say. You

shall swear to abide by this oath. "I'll have nothing to do with lover or husband...."

Calonice: "I'll have nothing to do with lover or husband...."

Lysistrata: "Even if he approaches me erectly." (Calonice is reluctant). Say it!

Calonice: "Even if he approaches me erectly." O Lysistrata, my knees are dissolving.

Lysistrata: "But I'll remain chastely at home...."

Calonice: "But I'll remain chastely at home...."

Lysistrata: "Wearing sensual garments...."

Calonice: "Wearing sensual garments...."

Lysistrata: "To excite my husband as much as possible...."

Calonice: "To excite my husband as much as possible...."

Lysistrata: "....and I'll never satisfy his desire...."

Calonice: "....and I'll never satisfy his desire...."

Lysistrata: "But if he tries to force me against my will...."

Calonice: "But if he tries to force me against my will...."

Lysistrata: "I'll clamp my legs together tightly...."

Calonice: "I'll clamp my legs together tightly...."

Lysistrata: "I won't spread my thighs for him...."

Calonice: "I won't spread my thighs for him...."

Lysistrata: "And I'll never get on top of him, no matter how big

he gets...."

Calonice: "And I'll never get on top of him, no matter how big

he gets...."

Lysistrata: "If I keep my vow, may I drink deeply...."

Calonice: "If I keep my vow, may I drink deeply...."

Lysistrata: "But if I break my oath, may the wine turn to

water...."

Calonice: "But if I break my oath, may the wine turn to

water...."

Lysistrata: Do you all swear?

Myrrhine: Yes!

Lysistrata: Then I'll start the sacrifice. (Drinks).

Calonice: Just drink your share, my dear, so there's enough to go around. (The women pass the bowl around. Women shout from offstage).

Lampito: What's that shouting?

Lysistrata: What I told you earlier! The women just captured the Acropolis. Hurry, Lampito, return to Sparta and prepare the women there for our plan. The rest of us can go to the Acropolis and help defend it against the men.

Calonice: Do you think the men will attack us?

Lysistrata: I'm not worried about them. Neither threats nor fire will force us to open the gates, except on the terms we mentioned.

Calonice: Never, by Aphrodite! Let's show them that our reputation for stubbornness is true. (Exit the Women. Enter the Chorus of Old Men).

Chorus of Old Men: Advance, Draces, keep moving, even though

your shoulder aches from carrying this newly cut

tree. Truthfully, there are many unexpected surprises

in this long life! Alas, Strymodorus. Who would have

imagined that the very women we support at home

would impudently capture the Acropolis, and bar the

doors on us? But let's rush to the citadel right away,

Philurgus, and pile a ring of logs around the

rebellious women and set fire to them with our

avenging hands. We'll burn Lysistrata first. By the

goddesses, she won't laugh at us while I'm still alive.

Not even Cleomenes, the Spartan King, who was the

first to capture our Acropolis, got away unpunished;

for we besieged him there for seven years and in the

end, despite all his rage and fury, he surrendered his

weapons to us. He left in rags; dirty, squalid,

unkempt and unwashed. How fiercely I led the siege

against that great warrior and his men; our troops

guarded the doors in ranks seventeen deep and

never slept. Then why shouldn't I be able to punish

these insolent enemies of gods and men? If I don't,

may the memories of our victory at Marathon grow

dim. But we must hurry up the steep road to the

citadel and drag this log ourselves, without the help

of pack animals. How heavily it weighs on my

shoulders. Nevertheless, we must go on and we must

keep the fire going, or once we reach our target we'll

find it's died out. (Blows on the coals). Cough!

Cough! Oh! Oh. What a cloud of smoke! Great

Heracles, how it stings my eyes, leaping out of the

pan to assault me like a mad dog! Move forward to

the citadel to protect the goddess Athena. When

could we have a better chance to defend her,

Laches? (Blows on the coals). Cough! Cough! Oh. Oh.

What a cloud of smoke! By the favor of the gods the

fire still burns. We should put our log down here,

make torches from the wood and set them on fire

from the charcoal pans; then we should use the log

as a battering ram to burst in the doors of the

citadel. If the women don't unbolt the doors at our

demand, we'll set the doors on fire and drive them

out with the smoke. Now put down the log. (Blows

on the coals). What a cloud of smoke! By the gods!

What dainty aristocrats will help with the log? What

a weight off my back. Let the coals burn bright and

set the torches blazing. Goddess of victory, help us

triumph over these audacious women in the

Acropolis. (Enter Chorus of Old Women from the

Acropolis).

Chorus of Old Women: Women, I think I see flame and smoke, as if

something's burning. We must hurry. Quick, quick,

Nicodice, before we're surrounded by these nasty

old men and set on fire because of their unjust laws.

That's what I feared. What if I'm too late to rescue

my friends? After all that trouble we had filling our

pitchers at the fountain because of the crowds of

gossiping women and pushy slaves. At last we're

here to save our friends. For I heard the boasts of

those foolish old men threatening to break down the

doors and swearing horrible oaths to burn the

women to ashes. O goddess Athena, may I never see

that happen, but instead let the women save Greece

and its people from the madness of war! That's why

we occupy your fortress, o guardian of our city.

Protect us from the men who wish to burn us.

Stratyllis: Let me alone! Help! Help!

Old Women: What's this? O wicked old men! Honest men would

never do anything so evil.

Chorus of Old Men: This is a surprise! Look! Here comes a swarm

of women rushing out to stop us. (They retreat a

little).

Old Women: Are you afraid of us? Do there seem to be a lot of us?

Well, you've only seen a few of our thousands.

Old Men: Well, Phaedrias, shall we allow them to babble like

that? Should we beat them across the backside with

our sticks?

Old Women: Let's put our pitchers down, so if they try to assault

us our hands will be free. (They put down their

pitchers).

Old Men: By Zeus, if we smack them in the jaw a few times

they'll be silent.

Old Women: Well then! Just try to hit me! I'll give you a chance.

But if you dare, I'll bite your balls off like a mad dog!

Old Men: Silence! Or I'll beat you to death!

Old Women: Come closer, and just dare touch Stratyllis with your little finger!

Old Men: What will you dare do if I thump her with my fists?

Old Women: I'll tear out your lungs and entrails with my teeth.

Old Men: There's no poet wiser than Euripides; for he knows there's no creature as shameless as woman.

Old Women: Rodippe, let's pick up the pitchers of water.

Old Men: O most hateful sluts, why did you come here with water?

Old Women: You old fool with one foot in the grave, why did you come here with fire, to cremate yourself?

Old Men: I'm going to build a funeral pyre and burn you and your friends.

Old Women: I brought water to douse the flames.

Old Men: You'd dare put out my fire?

Old Women: Soon you'll see.

Old Men: I should fry you with this torch right now.

Old Women:	If you brought some soap we'd give you a bath.
Old Men:	You shameless creatures want to wash me?
Old Women:	We'll clean every little part of you.
Old Men:	Did you hear her insolence?
Old Women:	I'm a free woman.
Old Men:	I'll make you mind your manners.
Old Women:	From now on you'll no longer be a juryman in the lawcourts.
Old Men:	Burn her hair!
Old Women:	Pitchers do your duty! (The Women pour water on the Men).
Old Men:	Ah, woe. What misery!
Old Women:	Was it too hot? (The Women pour more water).
Old Men:	It's freezing! Won't you stop? What are you doing?
Old Women:	I'm watering you so you'll grow.
Old Men:	But I'm shriveled enough with old age and I'm trembling from head to foot from that cold bath.

Old Women: Since you brought fire, warm yourself.(Enter Magistrate with Scythian Guards).

Magistrate: Have these wanton women erupted again in ritual drum playing and orgies, and mourning for the death of Adonis? When Demostratus, may plague take him, was in the assembly arguing for sending soldiers to Sicily, his drunken wife was dancing on the roof, crying: "Alas! Alas, for Adonis!" Demostratus argued to enlist Zacynthian hoplites, curse him, while his wife was weeping for Adonis. Then that mad beast, hateful to the gods, persuaded the assembly to send our men, bringing us disaster. Such is the wantonness of women.

Old Men: What would you say if you heard more of the insolence of these hags? They've insulted us and drenched us with water, so we're wringing our clothes as if we pissed in them.

Magistrate: And well earned, by Poseiden! For when we join the

women in immoral acts and teach them to be

licentious, we get what we deserve. One man goes to

the jeweler's and says: "While my wife was dancing

last night the clasp of her necklace fell out of the

hole. I'm going away on business, but I want you to

come by tonight and put a large pin in the open

clasp." Another man goes to the shoemaker, a young

lad, but able to do a man's job, and says: "A strap is

pinching the tender little toe of my wife's foot. Visit

her while I'm at the lawcourt and loosen it, so it

spreads wider." Then the same kind of thing happens

to a magistrate. When I come here to get money to

pay sailors those insolent women bar the gates. But

there's no time to stand around doing nothing. Fetch

a lever and force open the gates, so I can punish

their audacity. (To the Chorus of Old Men). What are

you gaping at, you wretch? And you, stop looking for

a tavern. Place a lever under the gates on that side.

My men and I will force this side open.

(Enter Lysistrata).

Lysistrata: Don't try to force your way in! I'm coming out

willingly. Why do you want levers? What we need

here is common sense and good judgement.

Magistrate: You vile creature! How dare you? Where are my

men? Arrest her and tie her hands behind her back!

Lysistrata: By Athena, if they touch me with one finger they'll

regret it, even though they're policemen! (Scythian

Guards slink back).

Magistrate: Are you men afraid? Both of you grab her around the

waist and quickly tie her.

1st Woman: By the goddesses, if you dare touch her we'll trample

you flat!

Magistrate: Flat you say! Where's another policeman? Tie this

instigator first!

2nd Woman: By Athena, if you just touch her, you'll need a doctor.

Magistrate: What's this? Where's that policeman? Arrest her! I'll

put down this rebellion.

3rd Woman: If you go near her I'll yank out every hair on your....

(Scythian Guards flee).

Magistrate: Woe is me! My men have deserted me. But we can't

let the women defeat us. (He coaxes Scythian Guards

back. They return). Form a battle line, my loyal

troops and advance against them!

Lysistrata: By the goddesses, you'll find out that there are four

companies of armed women inside!

Magistrate: Tie their hands, men! (Scythian Guards grab them).

Lysistrata: O women allies, come out! Market women and fish

wives! Attack! Smite, beat, push, insult them! Be

bold! (Women rush in and drive off Scythian Guards.

Exit Scythian Guards). Stop! Come back! Don't rob

them once they're beaten.

Magistrate: What shame! How poorly my men fought.

Lysistrata: What did you expect? Did you think you were

attacking mere slave-girls? You didn't know the

determination of free-born women.

Magistrate: Yes, by Apollo, if you visit a tavern first!

Old Men: Magistrate, you've wasted a lot of time talking while

on official business. Why bother conversing with

these wild beasts? Don't you see what a drenching

these hags gave us?

Old Women: But my good sir, you shouldn't assault your

neighbors. If you try again we'll blacken your eyes.

For I'm willing to stay modestly at home like an

innocent virgin, offending no one and not stirring a
limb. But if you shake me like a wasp's nest I'll fly out
and sting you.

Old Men: By the gods! What shall we do with these shameless
monsters? They're unbearable. But we must
investigate this case and find out why they captured
the sacred enclosure of the Acropolis. Question
everyone. Don't be deceived by them, for it would be
disgraceful to leave this situation unresolved. Do
your duty.

Magistrate: Well by Zeus, the first thing I want to know is why
you barricaded yourselves in our citadel.

Lysistrata: To capture the money, so it wouldn't be used to pay
for more fighting.

Magistrate: Do we fight because of money?

Lysistrata: Certainly. And all our other troubles are caused by
money. For our leaders want more and more money

for themselves and they don't care about the

suffering of the people. But they won't steal the

state's money any more!

Magistrate: What will you do with it?

Lysistrata: You really want to know? We'll take charge of it.

Magistrate: You'll take charge?

Lysistrata: Why are you so surprised? Don't we manage all

domestic affairs?

Magistrate: That's different.

Lysistrata: Why?

Magistrate: We need this money to pay for the war.

Lysistrata: But there's no need for war.

Magistrate: How shall we defend ourselves?

Lysistrata: We'll defend you.

Magistrate: You?

Lysistrata: Yes, us.

Magistrate: Then we're lost!

Lysistrata: Don't worry. We'll protect you, whether you like it or not.

Magistrate: This is outrageous!

Lysistrata: You're upset. Nevertheless, that's what must be done.

Magistrate: It's unfair!

Lysistrata: We must protect you, my friends.

Magistrate: Against our will?

Lysistrata: That makes it even more important.

Magistrate: Since when do women care about war and peace?

Lysistrata: I'll tell you.

Magistrate: (gesturing with fist). Tell me quickly, so you avoid a beating.

Lysistrata: Then listen and don't threaten!

Magistrate: I'm furious and I can't control myself!

Woman: Then you'll suffer even more.

Magistrate: (to Woman). Stop croaking at me, you old hag. (To Lysistrata). Go on with your story.

Lysistrata: During this long war and the war before it we modestly accepted everything the men did, for you never allowed us to express an opinion. But we understood you and often when you discussed affairs of state at home we realized that you managed many important affairs badly. Then, concerned with our country's fate, we'd ask with a loving smile: "What did you decide today in the assembly? Will you make peace?" "What's that to you?", you'd say: "Keep quiet." And we'd be quiet.

Woman: I'd never have kept quiet.

Magistrate: Then you'd have howled in pain.

Lysistrata: So I remained silently at home. I'd hear of a wicked new law and ask my husband: "Why do you manage the affairs of state so foolishly?" Then he'd look indignant and tell me: "Tend to you knitting or you'll weep with regret. War is men's business."

Magistrate: By Zeus, well said!

Lysistrata: Well said, you wretch? When you wouldn't let us advise you when all your plans were going wrong? But when we heard you asking in the streets: "Is there no real man to save the country?" and another answered: "No, not one!" Then an assembly of women immediately decided to act together and save Greece. Therefore, if you're willing to take our advice and be silent as we were, we'll solve all your problems.

Magistrate: You'll solve our problems? This is disgraceful and intolerable.

Lysistrata: Hold your tongue!

Magistrate: May I perish miserably if I hold my tongue for a woman wearing a veil

Lysistrata: If that's all that's bothering you, here! Take this veil

and wrap it around your head and hold your tongue.

Take this little shopping basket, adjust your garments

and do women's chores! From now on war is

woman's business.

Chorus of Women: Women, put down your pitchers so we may

help our friends. I never tire of dancing and never let

weariness bend my knees. I'm willing to risk

everything with these splendid women who are

intelligent, graceful, bold, wise, prudent and patriotic

in a righteous cause that will save the state. Come

Lysistrata, bravest of descendants of wise

grandmothers and prickly nettles, advance boldly

and don't give in! For the winds of fortune are

blowing our way.

Lysistrata: If the goddess of love makes our breasts and thighs

comely and stirs the men with erections, soon all

Greece will call us peacemakers.

Magistrate: How will that happen?

Lysistrata: First we'll stop armed men from loafing in the

marketplace and being disorderly.

1st Woman: Yes, by Aphrodite!

Lysistrata: For now they strut through the marketplace like

savages, armed from head to foot.

Magistrate: Yes, by Zeus! It shows their manliness.

Lysistrata: But it looks ridiculous for a ferocious fellow with a

huge shield and sword to buy a fish.

1st Woman: I saw a long-haired cavalry officer sitting on his horse

buy pea soup from an old woman and eat it from his

helmet. I saw another soldier shake his spear and

shield to frighten a fruit-seller, then steal the ripest

figs and devour them.

Magistrate: How will you bring peace and tranquility to our

disturbed country?

Lysistrata: Easily.

Magistrate: How? Tell us!

Lysistrata: Just as when our thread is tangled we work it in and

out until it's unsnarled, we'll end this war by sending

ambassadors all over the country to negotiate the

issues.

Magistrate: Do you think you can solve our terrible troubles with

knitting needles, you silly featherheads?

Lysistrata: Yes, and if you had any sense you'd administer the

affairs of state as well as we manage our knitting.

Magistrate: How then? Show me!

Lysistrata: First, just as you wash the dirt from virgin wool, whip

the scoundrels out of the city who stick to us like

briers. Next, tear to pieces those who conspire

together and pluck bald those who get official

positions illegally. Then put all the public good will into a basket adding citizens, strangers, resident aliens, friends, debtors, cities, states, allies; gather them into one great ball of wool and from it weave a cloak for all the people.

Magistrate: Isn't it shameful that these women should debate the issues when they're not involved in the war at all?

Lysistrata: What! You cursed man, we bear twice the responsibility that you do, since we bear sons who become soldiers who you send to be slaughtered.

Magistrate: Be quiet and don't remind us of our troubles!

Lysistrata: Second, while we're still young women and should enjoy the pleasures of youth, we sleep alone because our husbands are fighting far away. But let me not discuss the married women; for I grieve more for the young virgins who grow old without a man.

Magistrate: Don't men grow old?

Lysistrata: It's not the same. When a man comes back from war,
even if he's a greybeard, he quickly marries a young
girl. But a woman's time is brief and if she doesn't
take advantage of it no one is willing to marry her.
Then she'll spend the rest of her life alone, looking
for omens that never send her a husband.

Magistrate: But if an old man can still get an erection?...

Lysistrata: Since you won't learn anything, why don't you drop
dead? You can purchase a coffin and have a funeral
feast. Cover yourself with this! (Drenches him with
water).

1st Woman: Take this from me! (Drenches him).

2nd Woman: Take this crown! (Drenches him).

Lysistrata: What's missing? What more to you want? Go to the
ferryboat for the dead! Charon is calling you and he
won't sail without you.

Magistrate: Isn't it shameful that I suffer these abuses? By Zeus,
I'll go back to the council and show my fellow
magistrates what you've done.

Lysistrata: Will you bring a complaint against us because we
didn't bury you properly? On the third day after your
death we'll bring sacrifices to your tomb. (Exit
Magistrate, Lysistrata).

Old Men: Free men can sleep no longer. Come, sirs, let's throw
off some clothing and get to the business at hand!
For I smell a plot to set a tyrant over us. I'm afraid
that Spartan soldiers hiding in some traitor's house
may have tricked our women, who are detested by
the gods, into seizing the treasury so I can't get the
pay I live on. It's truly shameful that these rebellious
women should dare advise us about war and try to
make peace between us and the Spartans, who are
as trustworthy as hungry wolves. Citizens, they've

done these things to tyrannize us! But they shall not oppress me, for I'll be on my guard. From now on I'll wear my sword and lounge in the marketplace in full armor, next to the hero's statue and pose beside him; for I too have a heroic destiny; to smack this abominable old hag in the jaw.

Old Women: Try to play the hero and your own mother won't recognize you. But dear women, let's shed our excess clothing. O citizens, we are starting a speech that will benefit the state which we wish to repay for raising us so well. From earliest youth through young womanhood I loyally served the state in traditional ways. Don't I then owe the state good advice? Don't begrudge my help because I'm a woman, if I have a better plan than the one you've already tried. For I am a contributor to the state; I contribute sons. But you miserable old men contribute nothing. After you waste your ancestral inheritance you drain the

income of the state. Now we're in danger of your

ruining it all. And you dare complain? If you annoy

me I'll smack you in the jaw with my slipper.

Old Men: Shall we endure this insolence? And I'm afraid things

will get worse. But whoever is endowed with a man's

parts will help me end this rebellion. Let's remove

more clothing, since it's right to smell like a man and

wrong to bind ourselves in a fig leaf. But now bold

warriors, just as we went eagerly to war in our youth,

we must become young again and shed the aches of

old age. For if we allow these women the smallest

advantage, nothing will stop their daring schemes

and they'll replace our knights. For women have

good seats and are skillful in horsemanship, and

won't slip and fall when galloping. Consider the

painting of the Amazon women fighting on

horseback with the men. But we should put their

necks into wooden collars.

Old Women: By the goddesses, if you provoke me I'll lose my

temper and you'll call your fellow tribesmen to save

you from a beating. Let's also take off more clothing

so we smell like passionate women and even bite

them. Now let any old gray-beard dare come near

me! He'll never eat garlic or beans again. If you dare

say anything bad about me, for I'm really furious

now, I'll swoop down on you like a wild eagle. For I

don't fear you as long as my allies Lampito and

Ismenia are alive. For you'll be powerless even if you

pass a decree seven times, you wretch, for you're

detested by all your neighbors. Only yesterday, when

I was sacrificing to the goddess, I ordered an eel from

Boeotia, but they refused to send it because of your

decrees! And you won't stop passing those decrees

until someone trips you and breaks your neck. (Enter

Lysistrata). O bold Queen who planned this deed,

why do you look so sad?

Lysistrata: The wicked behavior of women and the weakness of

the feminine mind have discouraged me.

Old Women: Why? What are you saying?

Lysistrata: The truth!

Old Women: What's disturbing you? Tell your friends!

Lysistrata: It's difficult to be silent, yet shameful to speak.

Old Women: Don't conceal the injury we've suffered.

Lysistrata: In a word, the women are overeager for sex.

Old Women: O Zeus!

Lysistrata: Why call Zeus? That's how things are. I can't keep the

women from their husbands; they keep sneaking

away. The first one I caught was digging a tunnel; the

second was lowering herself down the wall with a

rope; a third was getting ready to desert; another

mounted a tiny sparrow and wanted to fly to her

husband's arms; I had to pull her back by the hair.

The rest keep making all kinds of excuses to go

home. Look! Here comes one now. Ho, you! Where

are you going? (A Woman attempts to run past).

1st Woman: I'm planning to go home, for moths are eating my

wool.

Lysistrata: What moths? Go back to your post.

1st Woman: By the goddesses, I'll come right back as soon as I

spread my wool on the couch....

Lysistrata: You're not spreading anything, or going anywhere!

1st Woman: Must my wool be ruined?

Lysistrata: If it's necessary. (Exit 1st Woman. Enter 2nd Woman).

2nd Woman: Woe is me! Alas for my unbrushed fur which I've left

neglected at home!

Lysistrata: See! Here's another going home to brush her fur!

Come back here you!

2nd Woman: I'll return as soon as I brush it.

Lysistrata: Don't brush it! For then everyone else will do it also.

                 (Exit 2nd Woman. Enter 3rd Woman).

3rd Woman: O kind goddess, delay my giving birth until I leave

                 this holy place.

Lysistrata: What nonsense is this?

3rd Woman: I'm giving birth right now.

Lysistrata: But you weren't pregnant yesterday.

3rd Woman: Today I am. Please, Lysistrata, let me go home and

                 send for the midwife.

Lysistrata: What a ridiculous story! What's this hard bulge?

3rd Woman: A male child.

Lysistrata: No, it's not! You've stuffed yourself with something

                 metal and hollow. We'll see what it is. (Opens her

                 garment). You wretched goose! You said you were

                 pregnant and it's just a helmet.

3rd Woman: I am pregnant!

Lysistrata: Then why the helmet?

3rd Woman: In case I give birth in the Acropolis. I can drop the baby in the helmet like a bird laying an egg in her nest.

Lysistrata: What are you babbling about? These are pathetic excuses. It's obvious what you're doing. You better wait until the helmet hatches.

3rd Woman: Since I saw the snake that guards the temple, I can't sleep in the Acropolis. (Enter 4th Woman).

Lysistrata: My dear women, stop your deceitful tricks! You want your husbands; but they want you even more! And I surely know that they're spending restless nights alone. But hold out, dear friends, just endure a little longer! For an oracle said that we'll prevail, unless we're confused by dissension. Shall I tell you what the oracle said?

Old Women: Tell us. Tell us.

Lysistrata: Quiet! "When the swallows gather in one place and

avoid the Hoopoes and abstain from the penis, the

evils of life shall depart and high- thundering Zeus

will place the higher under the lower...."

Old Women: Will we lie on top?

Lysistrata: "But if the swallows disagree and fly away from the

sacred temple, they'll be the most shameful birds of

all."

Old Women: By Zeus, the meaning is clear!

Lysistrata: By all the gods, although we're suffering, let's go

back inside. For it would be disgraceful to betray the

oracle. (Exit Lysistrata).

Old Men: I want to tell you a story that I heard when I was a

boy; "There was once a young man named Melanion

who didn't want to marry, so he ran away to the

mountains. He had a dog and lived on rabbits

trapped in a net. He detested women so much that

he never went home again. And we who are chaste

men, detest women as much as Melanion."

Old Man: I want to kiss you, old woman....

Old Woman: You won't need an onion to make you cry.

Old Man: ...and spread your legs and step on you.

Old Woman: You have a dense forest there.

Old Man: Myronides had virile parts and a filthy, hairy ass that

frightened his enemies. So did Phormio.

Old Women: I want to reply to your story about Melanion. There

was a coarse fellow named Timon, wild and unruly,

whose face was surrounded by an unapproachable

thorny beard, a true descendant of the Furies. Timon

hated wicked men and ran off to the mountains

cursing your evil ways; but he was always gentle with

women.

Old Woman: Would you like a smack in the jaw?

Old Man: By no means! You're frightening me!

Old Woman: Then I'll kick you.

Old Man: You'll expose your garden.

Old Woman: But you won't see any unseemly hair even though

I'm an old woman, because I burned it off with a hot

lamp. (Enter Lysistrata with several women).

Lysistrata: (from the wall of the Acropolis). Ho there, Women!

Come here quickly!

1st Woman: What's the matter? Why are you calling us?

Lysistrata: I see a man with a big erection approaching, aroused

by the passions of love. O goddess, help us keep our

resolve!

1st Woman: Where is he, whoever he is?

Lysistrata: Coming closer.

1st Woman: You didn't exaggerate! Who is he?

Lysistrata: Look! Does anyone know him?

Myrrhine: I do! He's my husband, Cinesias.

Lysistrata: It's your duty to excite, torment and completely

                thwart him; tantalize him; let him see what he wants,

                but don't let him get it. Tempt him, but keep your

                legs closed.

Myrrhine: Don't worry; I'll do it.

Lysistrata: I'll stay here and make sure things go smoothly. The

                rest of you go in. (Exit Myrrhine, Women. Enter

                Cinesias, Servant, Child).

Cinesias: Woe is me! My pole is so stiff that it's pointing like a

                hunting dog!

Lysistrata: Who's approaching our guardposts?

Cinesias: I am.

Lysistrata: Are you a man?

Cinesias: Of course I'm a man.

Lysistrata: Then depart.

Cinesias: Who's chasing me away?

Lysistrata: I'm the sentry for the day.

Cinesias: By the gods, I beg you, call Myrrhine!

Lysistrata: Why should I call Myrrhine? Who are you?

Cinesias: Her husband Cinesias, always erect and ready.

Lysistrata: Welcome, dear man! Your name is not unknown to

us. You're constantly on her tongue; and if she puts

an egg or apple in her mouth, she says, "I wish it was

Cinesias!"

Cinesias: Please call her!

Lysistrata: Will you give me something if I do?

Cinesias: Yes by Zeus! Something big and firm, if you like.

Lysistrata: I'll hurry and call her.

Cinesias: Go quickly then! (Exit Lysistrata). There's no delight

in life since she left the house. I'm miserable

whenever I'm there, because the place always seems

deserted. And there's no pleasure in eating or

drinking, for I've got an erection all the time and it's

starting to hurt.

Myrrhine: (Talking to Lysistrata in the Acropolis above). I love

him! I love him! But he doesn't love me! Don't make

me see him!

Cinesias: My dearest little Myrrhine, why do you talk like that?

Come down to me!

Myrrhine: By Zeus, I won't!

Cinesias: Won't you come down if I coax you, Myrrhine?

Myrrhine: No! For you don't want me!

Cinesias: Not want you? I'm bursting my clothes for you!

Myrrhine: I'm going now.

Cinesias: Don't go, please! At least listen to your helpless

child! (To the Child). Wake up, you! Call your mother!

Child: Mama! Mama! Mama!

Cinesias: Won't you answer him? Don't you pity this neglected

waif, not fed or washed for six days?

Myrrhine: I pity him for having such a negligent father.

Cinesias: Come down to your little child, sweetest of women!

Myrrhine: What a burden it is to be a mother! I must go to him.

What else can I do? (Enter Myrrhine).

Cinesias: She seems to be much younger and more beautiful,

and she's so angry and aloof that I'm aching with

desire for her.

Myrrhine: O sweetest child of a terrible father! Come to me and

let me kiss you, dearest of all to me!

Cinesias: O heartless woman, why did you join the other

women and make both of us miserable?

Myrrhine: Don't touch me!

Cinesias: Our house is falling apart because of you.

Myrrhine: I don't care!

Cinesias: Don't you care about your wool that's being

destroyed by the chickens?

Myrrhine: Not at all!

Cinesias: We haven't celebrated the rites of Aphrodite for a

long time. Won't you come home?

Myrrhine: Not I, by Zeus! Not unless you end the war and make

peace.

Cinesias: If it seems best to you we'll do it.

Myrrhine: If it seems best to you I'll come home; after you

make peace!

Cinesias: At least lie down beside me for a little while.

Myrrhine: Certainly not! Though I won't say that I don't love

you.

Cinesias: You do love me? Then why won't you lie down, my

little Myrrhine?

Myrrhine: O you foolish man! In front of the child?

Cinesias: No, by Zeus! Manes, take him home! (Servant leads

child out). There! He's gone! Now lie down.

Myrrhine: Right here in the open, you dolt?

Cinesias: Where? Near the temple?

Myrrhine: Then I wouldn't be pure.

Cinesias: You could purify yourself by washing in the fountain.

Myrrhine: Do you want me to break the sacred oath I swore,

              you rascal?

Cinesias: Let the blame fall on me! Don't worry about your

              oath!

Myrrhine: Well then let me fetch a comfortable, little bed for

              us.

Cinesias: The ground is good enough for us.

Myrrhine: By Apollo, I won't let you lie on the hard ground,

              even if you're a wretch. (Exit Myrrhine).

Cinesias: It's plain to see that she adores me.

Myrrhine: (returns with a rope pallet). Here! Lie down quickly

              and I'll undress. (Cinesias lies down on the pallet). Oh

              dear! I must get a mattress.

Cinesias: We don't need a mattress!

Myrrhine: Yes we do! It would be shameful to lie on those old

              ropes.

Cinesias: At least let me kiss you!

Myrrhine: There! (Kisses him and exits).

Cinesias: Oh! Come back quickly!

Myrrhine: (returns with mattress). Here's a mattress! Lie down!

               I'll undress. Oh dear, you don't have a pillow.

Cinesias: I don't want one.

Myrrhine: But I do! (Exits).

Cinesias: Will she entertain my penis like a hero?

Myrrhine: (returns with pillow). Get up! Lift your head!

Cinesias: I have everything I need.

Myrrhine: Yes, everything.

Cinesias: Come to me my little treasure!

Myrrhine: Now I'll get undressed! But remember; don't deceive

               me about ending the war.

Cinesias: May I perish if I do!

Myrrhine: You don't have a blanket.

Cinesias: I don't want a blanket! I want sex!

Myrrhine: Don't worry. You'll get it. I'll be right back. (Exits).

Cinesias: This woman will kill me with bedding.

Myrrhine: (returns with blanket). Stand up!

Cinesias: I'm standing up already.

Myrrhine: Would you like me to oil you?

Cinesias: Definitely not!

Myrrhine: I will, whether you like it or not! (Exits).

Cinesias: O Zeus, may another liquid flow soon!

Myrrhine: (returns with jar). Hold out your hand; rub some on.

Cinesias: By Apollo, this stuff stinks! It won't help us celebrate

              our reunion.

Myrrhine: (Myrrhine sniffs the oil). Oh dear! I brought vinegar

              instead of oil.

Cinesias: That's all right. We don't need it, o my goddess.

Myrrhine: Don't be silly. (Exits with jar).

Cinesias: May whoever first discovered oil perish miserably!

Myrrhine: (Returns with new jar). Take this jar!

Cinesias: I have a better one here! Come here, you little tease.

Lie down and don't bring me anything else!

Myrrhine: I'm coming! Close your eyes! Now don't forget to

vote for peace.

Cinesias: I'll do it. (Exit Myrrhine). My wife has killed me,

building me up then letting me down. Alas! What

shall I do? How can I relieve my anguish now that I've

lost the most beautiful woman? Can I train myself to

wait? There must be some way to get satisfaction!

(Enter Chorus of Old Men).

Old Men: O unhappiest of men, this cruel deception afflicted

your noble parts with dreadful suffering. How I pity

you. Alas! Alas! What kidneys could endure such

stress? What brave bowels and buttocks! What loins

could survive the strain of no release from morning

through night?

Cinesias: By Zeus, what painful spasms.

Old Men: This is what your scheming and detestable wife has

                done to you.

Cinesias: Don't say that! She's the sweetest and dearest of all!

Old Men: Don't drivel about sweetness! She's the vilest of the

                vile! (Exit Cinesias). O Zeus, if only you'd pick her up

                with a great whirlwind, turn her upside down, then

                let her fall to earth again and land on a stiff

                welcoming committee! (Exit Chorus of Old Men.

                Enter Spartan Herald and Magistrate).

Herald: Where is the Athenian Senate, or the Magistrates?

Magistrate: Are you a man or a satyr?

Herald: By the gods, young man, I'm a herald! I've come from

                Sparta to start negotiations.

Magistrate: Are you carrying a spear under your cloak?

Herald: No, by Zeus!

Magistrate: Why are you turning away? Why are you covering

                yourself with your cloak? Are your private parts

                swollen from the tensions of your journey?

Herald: The fellow's a rude lout.

Magistrate: You've got an erection! You dirty brute!

Herald: No I don't! Don't babble nonsense!

Magistrate: What's this here?

Herald: A Spartan proclamation case.

Magistrate: So is this. But tell me the truth, man to man. How are

                things in Sparta?

Herald: All Sparta is erect! So are our allies. We can't even

                get prostitutes.

Magistrate: Did this punishment come from the gods?

Herald: No. Lampito started it; then the other women quickly

                followed her example and chased their husbands out

                of bed.

Magistrate: How are things now?

Herald: We're in distress. Everyone's walking around the city

              trying to hide their erections. For the women won't

              let us touch them until we make peace.

Magistrate: The women everywhere have sworn to deprive us.

              This proves it! Go back to Sparta and tell them to

              send ambassadors with complete authority to make

              peace! I'll tell the Senate about your condition and

              request them to appoint our ambassadors.

Herald: Agreed! I'll fly back! (Exit Herald & Magistrate. Enter

              Chorus of Old Men and Chorus of Old Women).

Old Men: Neither wild beast nor fire are more unconquerable

              than woman. Her ferocity puts the panther to

              shame.

Old Women: If you're aware of this, why do you make war on us,

              you wretch, when we could be true friends?

Old Men: I'll never stop detesting women!

Old Women: As you wish. But I won't let you run around naked.

              See how ridiculous you look! Let me come closer and

              help you on with your clothes!

Old Men: By Zeus, you did that nicely! I undressed in a blind

              rage.

Old Women: Now you look manly, and not the least bit ridiculous.

              If you won't hurt me I'll help you remove that beastie

              in your eye.

Old Men: That's what's been bothering me! Here! Take it out

              and show it to me. It's been stinging me for a long

              time.

Old Women: I'll do it; even though you're a grumpy man. O Zeus!

              There's a gigantic insect in your eye. Don't you see it?

              It's huge!

Old Men: By Zeus, you've saved me; for it was digging deep

              wells in me. Not that it's out my tears are flowing

              copiously.

Old Women: Now I'll clean you, although you're very naughty;

then I'll kiss you.

Old Men: Don't kiss me!

Old Women: I will! Whether you like it or not!

Old Men: Plague take you! You're a manipulator by nature!

There's a well known saying: "We can't get along

with you, yet we can't get along without you." But

now let's make friends and I'll treat you well, and you

do the same. Come, let's sing a celebration song

together!

Old Women: Honored audience, we don't want to say bad things

about any citizen. We want to speak well about

everyone and forget everything bad. We suffer

enough as it is. But let everyone know that if they're

poor and need money to live we have enough to

share with them. And if ever there's peace in our

land whoever takes money now need not repay it

later. We're going to entertain some travelers with a splendid feast, so you'll all eat well. Come to my house today! But first go to the public baths and also wash your children. Then come to the feast without asking anyone's permission to enter, but boldly take your place as if you were at home, for the door will be closed. (Exit Chorus of Old Women).

Old Men: Look! Here come the Spartan ambassadors, wearing some kind of bandage around their legs. (Enter Spartan Ambassadors). Welcome, Spartans! What condition are you in?

Spartan: There's not much to say. You can see for yourself.

Old Men: By the gods! Your condition is definitely expanded! It's tremendously inflamed.

Spartan: Terribly! What can I say? By all means let your ambassadors join us and make peace on whatever terms they like.

Old Men: These men are standing stiffly at attention as if ready

                for a ceremony. I see our men approaching. (Enter

                Athenians).

Athenians: Where's Lysistrata? For we've come here in a rigid

                condition.

Old Men: Both Spartans and Athenians have the same disease.

                Do you get up in the morning with a stiff ache?

Athenians: No, by Zeus, but I'm dying from the strain of

                supporting this growth. If someone doesn't make

                peace soon, I'll rape the prettiest man in sight.

Old Men: If you're smart you'll adjust your clothes and disguise

                your problem before someone mutilates you.

Athenian: That's good advice!

Spartans: By all means! Let's cover ourselves!

Athenians: Welcome, Spartans! We've suffered shameful things.

Spartans: Dearest of friends! We'd have suffered worse if we

                were caught standing up like this.

Athenians: Well now, Spartans, one thing at a time. Why are you

here?

Spartans: To make peace.

Athenians: Well said! That's why we're here. Let's call Lysistrata.

She's the only one that can make peace between us!

Spartans: By the gods, agreed!

Old Men: We don't have to call her. Look! Here she comes

after overhearing everything! (Enter Lysistrata). Hail!

Bravest of women. Now you must be clever, honest,

serious, gentle and shrewd. For the leaders of

Greece, captivated by your charm, have given you

power to settle their grievances.

Lysistrata: That would be very easy if everyone really wanted

peace and wasn't just deceiving each other. But I'll

soon find out. Go fetch the goddess of Peace. First

bring the Spartans forward, politely and kindly, not

like our clumsy husbands; but respectfully, like

proper women. And if someone is reluctant to give you his hand, lead him by the penis. (Enter Peace, represented by a beautiful woman). Pay attention! Now lead the Athenians forward by the easiest part you can grab. Spartans stand to my right and Athenians to my left and listen carefully! It's true that I'm a woman, but I'm well endowed with common sense and intelligence. By listening attentively to my father and elders discussing the affairs of state, and other subjects, I became well educated. I must blame both sides, who worship the same gods the same way. How many other similarities could I mention if I wanted to? Yet you're destroying each other, while barbarians wait everywhere to destroy us. That's my first point.

Athenians: I'm dying with desire.

Lysistrata: Now it's time to discuss the Spartans. Do you remember when a Spartan king came to Athens as a suppliant; and sat before our altars begging for help from our army? At that time your helot slaves were in revolt and there was also a terrible earthquake that devastated your land. But our men went to your aid with an army of 4,000 and saved Sparta. So why do you devastate our land after we helped you?

Athenians: By Zeus, Lysistrata, they're wrong to do that!

Spartans: We're wrong! But what a beautiful ass! (Referring to Peace).

Lysistrata: Now it's the Athenians turn. Don't you remember when the Spartans aided you against the tyrant of your city who enslaved you? And fought by your side and freed you, so now you wear the garments of free men rather than the rags of slaves?

Spartans: I've never seen a nobler woman!

Athenians: I've never seen nobler breasts!

Lysistrata: Then why, when you've done so much good for each

               other, do you still persist in fighting this wicked war?

               Why don't you make peace? What's stopping you?

Spartans: We're willing, if they're willing to restore a little

               morsel.

Athenians: Which one, honorable sir?

Spartans: The city of Pylos, which we've wanted for a long

               time.

Athenians: By Poseidon, absolutely not!

Lysistrata: Concede it to them, noble sirs!

Athenians: What do we get?

Lysistrata: Ask for something else in exchange!

Athenians: Then give us, how do you describe these two

               mounds, the curved gulf behind and the legs of

               Megara!

Spartans: No, by the gods. Never, good sir!

Lysistrata: Give them up! Don't quibble about legs!

Athenians: Now I'll take off my cloak and plow immediately.

Spartans: By the gods, I'll fertilize it right now!

Lysistrata: And you will! After you make peace. So if you think

this is the right thing to do, deliberate, then go

consult your allies.

Athenians: We don't need our allies! We're all aroused. They're

as excited as we are. We all agree. We need relief!

Spartans: So do we!

Athenians: All our allies agree!

Lysistrata: Well said. Now bathe and purify yourselves and we

women will entertain you with a great feast at the

Acropolis. Afterwards, you'll swear oaths and

exchange pledges to keep the peace; then each man

will go home with his wife.

Athenians: Let's go right away!

Spartan: Lead us wherever you want!

Athenians: Quickly! Quickly! (Exit Lysistrata, Athenians,

Spartans. Enter Chorus of Old Women).

Old Women: I don't begrudge offering my bedclothes, cloaks,

gowns, golden ornaments, all that I own to needy

children. I offer you the choice of anything you find

in my house and you won't find anything! Unless you

have better eyes than mine. If your servants and

children are hungry I'll give you wheat and fresh

bread. Therefore, let any poor person come to my

house and my servant will fill their sacks. But I warn

the worthless louts who loaf in the marketplace not

to come, for I'll set the dogs on them. (Exit Chorus of

Old Women. Enter Market Loafers who knock at the

door of the citadel).

Market-Loafers: Open the door!

Servant: (Enters with torch). Go away! What do you want? Do you want me to burn you? This duty of guarding the door is very trying.

Market-Loafers: I wont budge! (Enter Chorus of Old Men).

Servant: Do you see what we have to put up with?

Old Men: So do we.

Servant: Get away from here! Or I'll pluck you bald. Go! So the Spartans may leave undisturbed after the feast. (Drives them out. Exit Market-Loafers. Enter an Athenian from the feast).

Athenian: What a feast! I've never seen anything like it. How charming the Spartans were. We Athenians were wittiest once we drank enough wine.

Old Men: Truly said. We Athenians don't have all our wits about us when we're sober. If the Athenians take my advice we'll only send drunken ambassadors on state business. For whenever we go to Sparta sober we're always expecting trouble, so we either don't listen to them at all, or we're suspicious of anything they say. Then later each of us describes things differently. But now everything we do together is pleasant. We can even praise the entertainers for a poor show. (Enter Market- Loafers, who try to go in the door).

Servant: Look! Here they come again! This is the last warning, you louts. Go!

Market-Loafers: We'll go now that the feast is over. (Exit Market-Loafers. Enter Spartans).

Spartans: Play the flute, so I can dance and sing a pleasant song praising the Spartans and Athenians.

Athenians: By the gods, let the flute play! For I'm delighted to see you dance.

Spartans: O muse, bring back the memories of my youthful exploits when the Spartans and Athenians united and conquered the Persians. What a great naval battle

there was at Artemisium, when the Athenians
destroyed the Persian fleet. And when Leonidas led
the Spartans at Thermopylae we Spartans awaited
our enemies like wild boars, sharpening our tusks;
sweat poured down our faces, other liquid ran down
our legs, for the Persian army was as numerous as
the sands on the shore. O virgin goddess, Artemis the
huntress, slayer of wild beasts, witness our truce so
we'll keep the peace for a long time. Now may
friendship flourish from our agreements and may we
avoid treachery.

Lysistrata: Since everything is settled let the Spartans and the
Athenians dance in honor of the gods, to celebrate
our good fortune. Let's never go to war again!

Athenians: Let the dance begin! Offer thanks to the gods!
Artemis and her twin brother Apollo, patron of the
dance; Dionysus, who cavorts with the wild

Maenads; fiery Zeus and his noble wife Hera; and all the other gods who shall witness this special Peace brought by Aphrodite! Join us Spartans and show your skill.

Spartans: May the spirit of the muse enter me now, praising the gods and our heroic ancestors. Dance on! Touching the ground lightly, like the divine choruses who please the audience with their graceful dance. Where the beautiful maidens frolic like young fillies at the riverside, shaking their long hair in the wind, as Maenads wave their wands in the wild revels of the wine-god. Tie your hair with a ribbon and lead the dance. Let's celebrate our peace treaty and praise the mighty goddess of love, who conquered all of us.

Sidewalks Theatre
PRESENTS
ARISTOPHANES'
LYSISTRATA
DIRECTED BY GARY BECK
OCTOBER 18 - NOVEMBER 19 ; WED. - SAT. 8:00 ; SAT. & SUN. 3:00
SIDEWALKS THEATRE, 40 West 27 Street, 3rd Floor, New York, NY 10001
(212) 481-3077

www.ingramcontent.com/pod-product-compliance
Lightning Source LLC
Chambersburg PA
CBHW050504160726
48003CB00001B/149